NASHO

THE NATIONAL SERVICE EXPERIENCE 1951 - 1972

EDITED BY

RONALD PARSONS

First published 2014

National Library of Australia Cataloguing-in-Publication entry:

Title:	Nasho - national service experience 1951-1972 / edited by Ronald Parsons.
ISBN:	9781925046519 (paperback)
Subjects:	National service--Australia--History.
	Draft--Australia--History.
	Australia--Armed Forces--Recruiting, enlistment, etc.
	Australia--Armed Forces--Military life.
Other Authors/Contributors:	
	Parsons, Ronald T., 1935- editor.
Dewey Number:	355.2230994

Typeset in Times New Roman 12pt.

Cover Design by Boolarong Press

Disclaimer: Every effort has been made to ensure that the content of this book is factual. The editor and publisher take no responsibility for any errors or omissions. However, if an error or omission has occurred the publisher will gladly correct, or include acknowledgement in, any future edition.

Front cover photo: 2 Platoon 'A' Coy, 11 NST Battalion Intake 1/59 Wacol (Qld). Courtesy R. Davies.

Published by Boolarong Press, Salisbury, Brisbane, Australia.

Printed and bound by Watson Ferguson & Company, Salisbury, Brisbane, Australia.

Dedicated to all Australian National Servicemen and in Memory of those who died

ACKNOWLEDGEMENTS

Special thanks to the Hon. Ian Macfarlane, Minister for Industry and Federal Member for Groom, for supporting this publication of the National Servicemen's Association of Australia (Qld) Inc., Toowoomba and District Branch.

In addition, the support and grant of $3,000 towards the cost of this book from the Australian Government under the *Saluting Their Service* commemorations program is gratefully acknowledged.

A big thank-you as well to Allen Callaghan, Joyce McNeil, Dr Noel Wallis and Hugh Williams for allowing us to incorporate excerpts from their published works into *NASHO - THE NATIONAL SERVICE EXPERIENCE 1951-1972;* to Linley Parsons for word-processing and Richard Games of Copylam Services for scanning the photographs.

We also wish to express our sincere appreciation to the following members and others who have contributed to the project in one way or another, namely:-

Lawrie Asgill, Carol Baldwin, Carl Blume, Vicki Brown, Leo Camm, Anthony Caruana, Brian Cunningham, Dean DaCosta,

Roland Davies, Alan Elworthy, Neal Freier, Frank Giles, Dennis Gillbard, Darryl Hutton, Tony James, Leon Jeffery, Ron Keelan, Bill Lane, Bob Lange, David Laws, George Lovett, Don Macleod, Kyle MacLeod, Lawrie Maher, Lt. Jay McDaniell, Gordon Meiklejohn, Bill Nimmo, Michael O'Dea, Joan O'Sullivan, Pat O'Sullivan, Bill Parry, Jennifer Parsons, Roy Payne, Terry Pears, Russell Rea, John Rickard, Les Robinson, David Ross, Bill Sanderson, Max Schmidt, Ken Shadie, Keith Shepherd, Jim Skinner, Brian Smith, Joanne Stephens, Bob Wade, Padre Matthew Weatherley, Peter Wedgwood, Don Weimer and Ian Williams.

Finally, we would be remiss if we omitted to record our gratitude to Dan Kelly and his team at Boolarong Press for their enthusiasm, guidance and professionalism in the production of this book.

CONTENTS

FOREWORD

Nashos. If you asked most people in our community about this word they'd readily agree they've heard of it.

When you dig a little deeper and ask a few more questions, you'll often find that the most resonant association that people have with the word Nashos is the idea of people doing their bit for our country.

And that's exactly what Nashos are. Australia's national servicemen were ordinary blokes called up for compulsory service in the Australian Defence Force between 1951 and 1972. Of the 287,000 who served, 212 made the ultimate sacrifice and 1479 were injured.

Nashos made an important contribution to our national Defence deployment and continue to serve an invaluable connection to our military history. Whether it's speaking to local school students, participating in Anzac Day or Remembrance Day services, or through books like this one, the story of our national servicemen forms an important part of building our country's history and our national character.

I have no doubt that everyone who reads it will enjoy the side of national service that it depicts, but will also finish the book with a deeper understanding of the contribution Nashos have made to our Australian Defence operations.

Ian Macfarlane MP

Federal Member for Groom

Minister for Industry

INTRODUCTION

What is a Nasho?

The Australian Oxford Dictionary defines Nasho as '1 compulsory military training as introduced under the National Service Act. 2 a person who undergoes this.'

There have been four periods of compulsory military training since Federation in 1901, two of them since the Second World War. In the 1951-1959 Korea period, all young men aged 18 had to register for National Service. Over 500,000 were eligible, however, less than half were actually called-up. The remainder were either declared medically unfit, were excluded by ballot towards the end of the period, or were excluded for 'conscientious' or other reasons.

In the 1965-1972 Vietnam era men 20 years of age were selected by having their birth date drawn out of a barrel. Around 63,790 out of the 761,854 who had their twentieth birthday during that period served their compulsory two years. These National Servicemen made up a large part of Australia's commitment to the Vietnam conflict and many died serving their country. Nashos also served in Malaya (now known as Malaysia), Borneo and Papua New Guinea during that period.

It is a sad fact that while Nashos were expected to fight for their country, they were not entitled to vote, or sign contracts. The voting age was lowered from 21 to 18 in 1973 – a year after National Service ended. Contract and Property Laws were State matters which the States and Territories changed between 1970 and 1977.

Nashos have been officially recognised by being awarded the Anniversary of National Service 1951-1972 Medal and the Australian Defence Medal. Their sacrifice is also commemorated by the National Service Memorial alongside The Australian War Memorial in Canberra, as well as various State and Local Memorials.

Ronald Parsons

1
COMPULSORY MILITARY TRAINING PRE-1951

NOEL WALLIS AND HUGH WILLIAMS

Under the general heading of Compulsory Military Training, certain categories need to be considered, namely:

a. Pre-World War 1 training.

b. Conscription for World War 1 overseas service.

c. World War 2 Militia.

d. National Service 1951-1959 (Army, Navy, Air Force).

e. National Service 1965-1972.

Compulsory military training for young men was first introduced in Australia in 1911. The matter had been agreed to in principle by the infant Commonwealth Government in 1907. However, because of national political uncertainty and a vocal minority opinion against such a program, the legislation was delayed for a few years. It was titled: The Defence Act 1903-1913 (amended).

The amended Bill required 'junior cadets' to perform ninety hours of service; 'senior cadets' four whole days plus twelve half days and twenty-four night drills. 'Citizen Forces' did sixteen whole days, or equivalent, including eight days in camps. Whilst there were some variations to the scheme's implementation, all young, fit males between the ages of 12 and 25 were required to do duty. Capt. Iver A. Williams, a participant in the scheme, explained it as follows:

'In 1911 compulsory military training for all males aged 14 to 26 (sic) was introduced. It was possibly the basis of the great reputation Australians earned in the First World War.

From ages 14 to 16 you were junior cadets and parades were for two hours each Thursday evening and three hours every 2nd Saturday – and it was real training.

Two Junior Cadets in camp with NSW Lancers, Pre-WWI training.
AWM AO5224

From 17 to18 you were senior cadets. Parades were two hours each Thursday evening and three hours every Saturday in four, from 9 am to 5 pm. All ranks gained in senior cadets were permanent and carried through to the citizen forces.

From 18 to 22 you were in the Citizen Military Forces. Parades were 2 hours per week of an evening, 3 hours every second Saturday afternoon and a full day one in four, plus ten days' camp per year.

From 22 to 26 you were on the reserve and did ten days' camp per year. The training throughout was hard, thorough and realistic.

Many employers did not like the scheme but they got used to it.'

Trainees retained civilian status and continued to work during their period of military service. Between 1911 and 1929 more than 636,000 were trained. The system was designed to train civilians in military techniques for use in defence of the homeland in time of need. Although such training is often referred to as 'conscription', especially in emotional debate, 'conscripts' usually become part of a standing army as full-time soldiers during their period of duty, and may serve at home or abroad, in peace or war, as part of that duty.

Even with conscription, Australia was unique in its original legislative provision that those 'conscripted' were for the defence of the country and would be confined to those territories under its authority. Conscription for overseas service failed to get off the ground during World War 1 as the two referenda that were held went against such a plan.

In World War 2 the Militia who went to New Guinea were still in 'Australian territory'. At no time in Australia's history, prior to the Vietnam conflict was our youth, strictly speaking 'conscripted' for overseas service beyond the provisions of the amended 1903 Act – as it is often called. The Act provided for compulsory military service in the time of war 'within the Commonwealth and any territory under the authority of the Commonwealth'.

The nearest we came to this was in 1943 when Prime Minister John Curtin's Government amended the Defence (Citizen Military Forces) Act to extend the limits of service as far as the equator and between longitudes 110 and 159 degrees east for the duration of the war plus six months. This extension still kept the spirit of previous legislation which forbade conscription for overseas service.

In passing, it should be noted that following the Declaration of World War 2 on 3 September 1939, the Menzies Government took steps to accelerate defence measures, and on 20 October introduced a scheme of three months' training for the voluntary Militia. This was extended by the calling-up of unmarried men attaining 21 years of age during the year ending 31 July 1940. Further classes of personnel were called-up in July and December 1940 and July and December 1941. Over 290,000 were called-up from 1939 to 1945. The period of training was increased progressively from 90 to 180 days per year. On winning power in October 1941, Curtin's Government called-up all members of the Militia for full-time training.

The transition from 'training' to 'service' for the Militia took place at the outbreak of war with Japan after Pearl Harbor in December 1941. Militia were stationed in Northern Australia and saw action in Darwin during the Japanese air raids on the city.

Who were the Militia? In the 1940's the term 'Universal Training Scheme' was applied to the calling-up of personnel under a national service order. These men were not called National Servicemen then but went by other names, some of which were derogatory. 'Chocko' (short for chocolate soldier) was one such name. At other times they were referred to as 'Uts' (universal trainees) and 'FIA' (forced into action) is said to have been used by opponents of conscription.

The first and greatest jungle operation in which Militia units fought side by side with soldiers of the AIF was the Battle for the Kokoda Track. Sometimes called the Battle of the Ranges as battle raged up and down the high, mountainous spine of Papua New Guinea. It lasted seven months, resulting in the defeat of the Japanese Army and ending the myth of Japanese infantry invincibility.

Australian Militia unit, Kokoda Track, 1942. *AWM O13289*

The Battle of Milne Bay (August 26 to September 6, 1942) also saw Militia involved with 'regulars' in conflict against the enemy. In this case the AIF troops were veterans of the Middle East campaigns. The compulsory enlistees (Militia) fought with great courage and distinction beside their more experienced comrades.

When World War 2 ended, compulsory military service was once more suspended. Prime Minister Chifley favoured air power as the main defence against growing post-war instability in the world.

Defence was a major issue in the 1949 election which resulted in a change of government. The coalition's policy was for the re-introduction of limited compulsory military service for the Army, Navy and Air Force should the need arise. That need arose sooner than expected.

POSTSCRIPT

The Japanese made three attempts to capture Port Moresby in World War 2. Their first attempt was by sea but was thwarted by the Battle of the Coral Sea in May 1942.

In July they next attempted to take Port Moresby by crossing the central massif from Lae and Salamaua along what Australians called the Kokoda Track, but due to American influence is now commonly known as the Kokoda Trail. (In another name change, when the Japanese finally surrendered, what was known as VJ Day, 'Victory' and 'Japan', was later changed to VP Day, 'Victory' and 'Pacific'.)

The following month the Japanese landed 2000 marines at Milne Bay. However, Australian regulars and militia inflicted on the Japs their first defeat on land in the war.

The Australian militia's fighting withdrawal and the subsequent successful offensive with AIF reinforcements on the Kokoda Track sounded the death knell for Japanese attempts to capture Port Moresby. Had the Japanese been able to take Port

Moresby, they would have had a strategic base from which to bomb or invade the east coast of Australia. – Ed.

1952 MESSAGE FROM MONTGOMERY OF ALAMEIN

NATIONAL SERVICE

A FEATURE ARTICLE by Field-Marshal The Viscount Montgomery of Alamein, KG, GCB, DSO.
(Specially written for THE NATIONAL SERVICE INFANTRYMAN)

I AM glad to have this opportunity of emphasising to you the importance of National Service. I believe that an adequate period of National Service is, today, vital to a nation which intends to defend its freedom.

For its defence a nation needs:

FIRST: Standing regular forces which actually exist in peacetime at an appropriate degree of readiness. These forces are formed from long service regulars and from those National Servicemen who have completed their basic training. In some cases they may be quite small.

SECOND: Reserve forces, which must also exist in peace and must be so organised that they can be produced quickly at the time they are needed: adequately trained and ready to fight.

No nation can afford today to maintain permanently under arms in peacetime large regular forces. It aims to maintain in peacetime those forces necessary for its problems at home and overseas, with a degree of readiness of each which is in keeping with their tasks.

Behind these forces maintained 'in being' in peacetime, there must be properly organised reserves, ready to take the field quickly in support of the peacetime forces.

In general terms, the true and ultimate strength of a nation depends on its trained reserves and on a sound plan for getting those reserves, and the national war machine, into action quickly.

The object of National Service is not only to provide sufficient manpower for the army in peace; it is also to provide a steady flow of trained and disciplined men into the reserve army.

It is the reserve forces that count in the end. These can only be provided by trained National Servicemen who, having completed their period of National Service with the colours, and returned to civil life, are then recalled for proper periods of refresher training every year. It is in these reserve forces, properly organised, that the strength of a nation lies.

Without National Service you cannot have good reserve forces; and without good reserve forces a nation cannot spring to arms quickly to defend itself and play its full part in the struggle.

You have a great tradition to maintain. The standards set by Australian troops at Gallipoli, and in France and Palestine in the World War I, and in the Desert, in Malaya and New Guinea in World War II, are not easy to equal. But I am confident you çan do it. The fighting qualities of Australian troops in Korea proves that the younger generation is living up to the reputation of the old.

Every member of a free nation owes something to the country of his birth. The freedoms and liberties which we now enjoy were not easily won. They were achieved by the sweat and blood of our forefathers, and they are endangered now by the threat of Communism.

We are sometimes inclined to take these freedoms for granted—the right to say and write what we think without fear of hindrance; the right to a fair trial by an impartial jury; the right to worship our God in whatever manner we please. These are our heritage and they are in danger. It is not merely a duty but a privilege to be ready to defend them.

Let me wish each one of you success and the best of luck. And if war comes, I am confident that you will prove, as your fathers did . . . "In defence immovable; in attack irresistible".

Montgomery of Alamein

Field-Marshal.

(Monty grew up in Hobart, Tasmania where his father served as Bishop for 12 years - Ed.)

(1952 Message)

2
NATIONAL SERVICE - A BRIEF HISTORY

ALLEN CALLAGHAN

National Service conscripts, 1950's. *Photo courtesy NSAA*

Between 1951 and 1972, a total of 287,000 young Australian men were called-up in two separate schemes for compulsory training in the Navy, Army and Air Force. Of them, 212 were killed and 1479 wounded on active service in Vietnam, Malaya and Borneo. National Service was part of Australia's defence preparedness for three decades

THE BACKGROUND

National Service was a product of the post-World War Two global and regional conflicts facing Australia. These began with the Berlin blockade by the Soviet Union in 1948, the first Arab-Israeli war the same year, Communist insurgencies in Malaya and Vietnam, Communist North Korea's invasion of South Korea in 1950, the Suez Canal crisis of 1956, confrontation with Indonesia in Borneo in 1963 and the Vietnam War. The threat of nuclear war hung over the entire world.

The outbreak of the Korean War in 1950, coupled with the Malayan Emergency and the Viet Minh uprising against the French in Vietnam, appeared to threaten Australia directly. Recruiting for the regular Armed Services proving insufficient, the Menzies Government re-introduced conscription which had ended in 1945. The legislation had bi-partisan political support.

National Service was in the Australian tradition since Federation in 1901 of volunteer forces for overseas service backed up by a pool of basically trained men in the Naval Reserve, the Citizens Military Forces and the Citizens Air Force. In the First Scheme from 1951 to 1959, National Servicemen could nominate a Service preference but in practice most were allocated to units near their homes. The Navy and Air Force gave preference to family of former personnel or members of Cadet units. Overseas service was automatic in the Navy and Air Force.

A major change for the Army was that National Servicemen were given the option, at call-up, to volunteer for service anywhere overseas if war occurred. Most Nashos volunteered. Further Corps training would have been needed. World War Two militia had been restricted to Australia and territories in the south-west Pacific. The Korean armistice was signed in 1953 and no new direct threats developed during that decade, so the basic role of National Servicemen was as reservists.

The Second Scheme from 1965 to 1972 for the Borneo and Vietnam wars involved two years full-time service integrated into expanded regular Army units, with overseas deployment where required.

THE FIRST SCHEME 1951-59

In the first National Service scheme between 1951 and 1959, all young men aged 18 were called-up for training in the Navy, Army and Air Force. A total of 227,000 served in 52 Intakes.

NAVY: A total of 6,862 National Servicemen did their training in Intakes named after Australian pioneers or explorers at *HMAS Penguin* in Sydney, *HMAS Cerberus* at Flinders Naval Depot on Westernport Bay in Victoria, *HMAS Lonsdale* in Melbourne and *HMAS Leeuwin* near Perth. Sea service was done on ships of the Fleet.

ARMY: The Army was allocated the largest proportion of men - about 198,000 - and formed ten National Service Training Battalions. The locations of the Battalions were: Queensland, 11 Battalion at Wacol; New South Wales, 12 Battalion at Singleton and Holsworthy, 13 Battalion at Ingleburn and 19 Battalion at Old Holsworthy and Holsworthy; Victoria, 14, 15 and 20 Battalions at Puckapunyal and Watsonia; South Australia, 16

Battalion at Woodside; Western Australia, 17 Battalion at Swanbourne; Tasmania, 18 Battalion at Brighton.

Naval Nashos, HMAS Penguin, 1954. *Photo courtesy (Mrs) V. Brown.*

The 11th Battalion with 1500 trainees at its peak, was the largest. It served Queensland and Papua New Guinea. Trainees from the northern rivers of New South Wales from Tweed Heads to Newcastle and the New England tableland were sent north to Wacol or south to Singleton and Sydney as required. Some National Servicemen from Canberra, Queanbeyan, Yass, Goulburn and other southern NSW centres trained at Puckapunyal in Victoria. Northern Territory and Broken Hill National Servicemen trained at Woodside in South Australia.

AIR FORCE: About 23,500 National Servicemen undertook their training in National Service Training Units and were allocated to Flights, corresponding to platoons, at the major air bases and depots throughout Australia, including Garbutt in Townsville; Toowoomba and Oakey on the Darling Downs; Amberley and Archerfield in Brisbane; Schofield, Richmond,

Rathmines, Williamtown, Bankstown, Forest Hill and Uranquinty near Wagga Wagga in New South Wales; Fairbairn in Canberra; Point Cook, Laverton, Frognall, Tottenham, Ballarat and East Sale in Victoria; Mallala near Adelaide, and Pearce and Merredin near Perth. Trainees from South Australia and Tasmania also went to Laverton.

National Service Instructors were drawn from all three Services and most had World War Two, Korean, Borneo or Vietnam combat experience. National Servicemen in both schemes received the standard basic training for all new recruits. In certain cases, equivalent training was recognised as National Service.

Nasho Drill Platoon, 13 Battalion, Ingleburn, NSW, 1955.
Photo courtesy L. Maher

Army National Servicemen training, Puckapunyal, Vic. 1950's.
Photo courtesy L. Maher

Private A. Callaghan cleaning .303 rifle, Wacol, 1958.

Photo supplied by NASHO NEWS Qld.

SERVICE NUMBERS

Navy National Service numbers were followed by NS (i.e. 4382NS) in sequence from the first Intake. An 'A' preceded Air Force numbers. In Army and Air Force numbers, the first digit (i.e. 2/771128 or A111409) usually indicated the State in which the trainee was called up: 1 Queensland, 2 New South Wales, 3 Victoria, 4 South Australia, 5 Western Australia, 6 Tasmania and 1 (later 8) Papua New Guinea. Some first scheme trainees from southern New South Wales had 3 prefixes and during the Vietnam-era some trainees were assigned numbers from other States. In Army numbers the second digit was always a 7. First scheme Army numbers had an oblique. Vietnam-era numbers did not.

TRAINING PERIOD

Under the *National Service Act 1951*, all young men turning 18 on or after 1 November 1950 were required to undertake 176 days standard recruit training in the Navy, Army and Air Force, followed by five years in their respective Reserves. The first call-up notices were issued on 12 April 1951 and the first National Servicemen, for the RAAF, marched in during July.

The Navy required its National Servicemen for 124 days continuous training, and then thirteen days training each year for four years in the Naval Reserve. Army trainees initially were required to serve 98 days continuous basic training followed by 78 days training in the Citizen Military Force over three years. Army Nashos without a unit near their home, if required, returned to the nearest base to complete their obligation. The Air Force required its trainees for a continuous 176 days.

Air Force Nasho W. Chadwick in Lincoln Bomber cockpit.
Photo supplied by NASHO NEWS Qld

Australians resident in Papua New Guinea could fulfil their obligation in Australia, or by six year's service in the Papua New Guinea Volunteer Rifles. In 1955 the Navy and Air Force reduced training to 154 days and discontinued National Service in 1957. In 1957, the Army reduced initial training to 77 days and part time service in the CMF to 63 days over two years. It also reduced the call-up through a birthday ballot from the second Intake of 1957. The last Intake of the first scheme was in August, 1959.

The Australian Government decided on 24 November 1959 to discontinue National Service and on 30 June 1960 all National Servicemen were declared to have honourably discharged their obligation.

Those in the first scheme did not see active service, except for those who enlisted and fought in Malaya, Korea, Borneo and Vietnam. National Servicemen were on Naval ships that visited Korean waters during hostilities. They also were at the atomic bomb tests in 1952 at Monte Bello Islands in Western Australia and in 1956 at Maralinga in South Australia. RAAF National Servicemen worked on aircraft that had flown through atomic clouds. National Servicemen were placed on alert as part of a wider standby for active service during the Suez Canal crisis in 1956 but the crisis passed.

THE SECOND SCHEME 1965-72

With the outbreak of Confrontation with Indonesia between 1962 and 1966 and the Vietnam War, recruiting again was insufficient and the Government introduced the *National Service Act 1964*.

In the second scheme, men aged 20 were selected by a birthday ballot for the Army. The Navy and Air Force did not use National Service for Vietnam. An alternative allowed those liable to conscription to elect, a year before the ballot, to fulfil their National Service obligation by six years service in the CMF. Some 35,000 did so until this option was abolished.

Between 30 June 1965 and 7 December 1972, a total of 63,735 were called up for two years full time service integrated into regular Army units. This was reduced to 18 months in 1971.

After twelve weeks initial training at 1 Recruit Training Battalion at Kapooka, NSW; 3 R.T.B. at Singleton, NSW; or 2 R.T.B. at Puckapunyal, Victoria; National Servicemen were assigned to the many different Corps. Most National Servicemen were allotted to the Infantry, enabling the Army to increase the Royal Australian Regiment to nine Battalions.

Artillery Trainees, North Head, NSW, July 1966. *Photo courtesy J. Rickard*

Of them, 150 served in Borneo in 4RAR and 21 and 22 Constructions Squadrons. Another 15,381 served in Vietnam. The remainder served in support units in Australia, Malaysia and Papua New Guinea.

A total of 1,639 completed officer training at Scheyville in Sydney and were commissioned as second lieutenants. Another 600 who were teachers were promoted to sergeant and posted to Papua New Guinea for 12 months to educate soldiers of the Pacific Islands Regiment at Port Moresby, Goldie River, Lae and Wewak. National Servicemen also served in PNG in Signals, Ordnance, RAEME, Small Ships, Surveying and other units.

During Confrontation with Indonesia between 1962 and 1966, the Government committed 3 and then 4 Battalion, Royal Australian Regiment, plus support units to Borneo. All Battalions were rotated through Vietnam between 1966 and

1971. Most but not all units gave National Servicemen the choice of active service and most volunteered. Of them, two died in Borneo and 210 in Vietnam. They included those who enlisted on or during call-up, or re-enlisted and voluntary National Servicemen.

7 Platoon 'B' Coy, 2 RTB Puckapunyal, Vic. Intake 1 March Out, 1971.
Photo courtesy Lt. J. McDaniell

The McMahon Government withdrew Australian units from Vietnam in 1971. In 1972, the Whitlam Government, using the expedient of *'exceptional hardship'*, discharged National Servicemen from the Army and passed the *National Service Termination Act* in 1973. The *Defence legislation Amendment Act of 1992* repealed the *National Service Act 1951* but the then Labour Government retained conscription in a time of war with prior Parliamentary approval.

NATIONAL SERVICE IN REVIEW

Australia has had compulsory training in the Citizens Military Forces at various times between 1910 and 1945. The 1951 and 1964 *National Service Acts* revived this with National Servicemen after their full time service, completing their obligation in their respective Reserves.

In 1974 the CMF was reorganised as the Army Reserve. The Citizens Air Force was absorbed into the Air Force Reserve. The Naval Reserve remained virtually unchanged. In 2001 the *Defence Act* was amended so that Reservists could be called up for overseas service.

Despite the compulsion, National Servicemen of both schemes did their training, active and reserve duties well and honourably and most regarded it as a rewarding part of their lives. They served overseas in Borneo, Vietnam, Malaysia and Papua New Guinea.

In 2001, the Australian Government recognised the contribution of National Servicemen to Australia's defence preparedness with the award of the *Anniversary of National Service 1951-1972 Medal.* The bronze medal is of double-sided design with the recipient's service number and name engraved on the rim. The front depicts the tri-service badge surmounted by the Federation star and the words *'Anniversary of National Service 1951-1972'* and the other side the Southern Cross on a field of radiating lines inside a cog wheel representing the integral role of the armed services in the Australian community. Both sides are surmounted by the Crown. The ribbon uses the colours of three Services during the National Service era - Navy white, Army jungle green and RAAF light blue - and Australia's then national colours of blue and gold. The ochre strip represents the land. In 2006, National Servicemen, along with all other servicemen and women, were awarded the *Australian Defence Medal.*

Because National Service was drawn from the entire community many National Servicemen from both schemes later rose to high positions in politics, business, the professions and the community. They include Governors-General Bill Hayden and Dr Peter Hollingworth; three Tasmanian Governors – Sir Guy Green, William Cox and Peter Underwood; deputy Prime Minister Tim Fischer and Federal Minister Wilson Tuckey; Victorian Premier Jeff Kennett; Queensland deputy Premier Sir Llew Edwards; Queensland Chief Justice Paul De Jersey; Major-General Rod Fay; businessmen Lindsay Fox and Sir James Hardy; television personalities Clive James and Graham Kennedy; entertainer Normie Rowe; AFL coach Kevin Sheedy; cricketer Doug Walters and car racing legends Peter Brock and Dick Johnson. There were Aboriginal, Torres Strait Islander and Pacific Islander National Servicemen.

However, the domestic divisions over the Vietnam War saw National Servicemen, particularly those who had active service, in the invidious position of not only being conscripted by a selective ballot but also subjected to public derision by some of the Australian public. This has made both sides of politics reluctant to consider National Service to supplement chronic shortfalls in voluntary recruiting.

All National Servicemen are ex-servicemen. They march on Anzac Day, Remembrance Day, National Service Day, Vietnam Veterans' Day and Reserve Forces Day in their own right. No women were called up for National Service. National Servicemen marched as a contingent in the Army's Centenary Parade in Canberra in 2001. They wear a wide variety of Service and Corps badges on their hats, caps and berets and many are members of Unit associations in all three Services.

The late Barry Vicary founded the National Servicemen's Association of Australia in Toowoomba, Queensland, on 28 November 1987 to seek a better deal for Vietnam-era National Servicemen and a medal recognising National Service. When Barry learnt of the earlier and larger National Service scheme he immediately widened the organisation to include them. The Association now has branches Australia-wide and is the second-largest ex-service organisation after the RSL.

National Servicemen added a new word to the Australian language – Nasho. National Service Day, 14 February, marks the day the last Nasho completed his obligation.

INGLEBURN

Tread lightly here;
Lest you arouse too poignant memories
Of men who met
The second threat
Of blood and sweat,
Aimed at Australia from across the seas.
They passed through here.

Tread proudly here.
The Southern Cross is blazing in the North;
And once again
Australian men
Are fighting. When
United Nations call they sally forth.
They go from here.

Tread gladly here.
The future brightens, for the thing you do
Will keep aglow
The torch we know
Was theirs; and so
Secure our freedom and ensure that you
Are happy here.

Tread humbly here.

No need to boast or vulgarly display
The things you've done,
The race you've run,
Or what you've won.
To those who ask you need but simply say:
You came from here.

This poem was written for regular and national service infantrymen, training for the Korean, and a possible 3rd World War, at Balikpapan (later Bardia) Barracks, Ingleburn NSW, in the 1950's. Poet unknown. – Ed.

SERVICEMEN'S
NATIONAL
ASSOCIATION
51
72
NAVY · ARMY · AIRFORCE

3
THE KOREAN WAR

RONALD PARSONS

Less than five years after the end of World War 2, war erupted on the Korean Peninsula when communist North Korean military forces crossed the 38th parallel and attacked non-communist South Korea.

It was June 1950 and at the time it was thought that it could be the start of a third World War between the communist countries and the West. There was also the threat that such a war could escalate into a nuclear Armageddon.

Closer to Australia the French were fighting communist forces in what was then Indo-China, a state-of-emergency had been declared in Malaya and there were communist uprisings in Burma, India, the Philippines and Indonesia.

Two days after the North Koreans launched their attack, the United Nations Security Council recommended that members of the UN assist South Korea, seeing that the invaders had failed to respond to a call for an immediate withdrawal.

A UN force was quickly assembled under the command of World War 1 and 2 veteran General Douglas MacArthur. Australia was one of the first nations to join with the Americans. At the time, Australia was the mainstay of the British Commonwealth Occupation Force (BCOF) in Japan with members of the Australian Army, Navy and Air Force still serving in southern Japan, not far from the ruins of Hiroshima. Over 36,000 Australian men and women served in the BCOF. Korea was only 200 kms away across the Sea of Japan.

MacArthur flew to Korea on 29 June and assessed the situation first hand. Until a substantial ground force could be landed it was planned to assist the retreating South Korean Army from the air and to place a naval blockade around the Korean Peninsula.

The Australian forces in Japan consisted of No.77 Squadron RAAF, 3 Battalion, Royal Australian Regiment and *HMAS Shoalhaven*. *HMAS Bataan* was en route to Japan.

Pusan was the major port on the south-east tip of the Korean Peninsula and it was there that UN Forces, which were mainly American, were landed. USAF B29 Superfortresses were ordered to bomb North Korean air bases while USAF and RAAF Mustangs, together with fighters from American and British aircraft carriers, attacked the North Korean ground forces and made short work of the North's Air Force.

With UN forces not fully deployed the North Koreans were able to compress the South Korean and UN ground troops into a tight perimeter around Pusan by early September, 1950. However, on the 16th of that month MacArthur turned the tables and landed his 10th Corps at Inchon, far behind the enemy lines. Inchon is the port for Seoul, the Capital of South Korea. By 27 September, Seoul was in UN hands.

3 RAR about to cross the 38th Parallel, Korea, 1950. *AWM HOBJ1484*

The landing at Inchon was a difficult operation and was opposed at first by the Pentagon and most of MacArthur's senior military advisors, particularly because of the tides which are the second highest in the world. However, MacArthur maintained that the North Koreans had made a grave error by neglecting their rear security and leaving their long supply lines vulnerable. This proved to be the turning point in the war. North Korean resistance was crushed. Attacked from front and rear with their supply line cut, it looked as if it was all over. But it was not to be.

Realising that communist North Korea was facing defeat in the northern autumn of 1950, China and the USSR came to their aid. Eight Chinese armies crossed the Manchurian border, while Russia supplied a substantial number of MiG-15 jet fighter aircraft to China to try and win back control of the airspace. Responding to the upgraded capacity of the Chinese Air Force, America replaced their Mustangs with Sabre jets while Britain supplied British Commonwealth Air Forces with Gloucester Meteor 8 jets.

Sgt. Pilot B.H. Collings (later Air Vice Marshall) of Toowoomba checking rockets under the wings of his Meteor Jet fighter, watched by LAC Howard Sharp of Brisbane. *AWM JK0755*

As fear of a Third World War heightened, the Menzies Government introduced National Service and all Australian males turning eighteen were required to register. Compulsory training was for all three services, though most were called up for the Army.

Meanwhile, by early December the last of the UN forces were withdrawing south of the 38th parallel. With the harsh Korean winter upon them the troops were suffering in the freezing winds. As temperatures plummeted, fingers stuck to the metal parts of small arms, hot coffee turned to ice in minutes, frostbite was common and medical problems multiplied.

In the spring thaw of 1951 the communists launched a major offensive which broke the UN defences. 3RAR which had been held in reserve was rushed forward, and supported by Canadian infantry and American tanks, held the key position of Kapyong for two days until the enemy force had spent itself. For this action 3RAR was awarded the US Presidential Citation.

So far No.77 Squadron, had in the nine months to April flown 3,872 operational sorties and lost 13 pilots. Squadron members had been awarded 70 decorations. The RAN during that period carried out escort and blockade duties as well as providing gunfire support for landings. Also in April 1951, 71 year-old General MacArthur was recalled and returned to America.

After their successful initial thrust the communist Chinese suffered disastrous battle losses in the first six months of 1951. So much so that they agreed to negotiations which took place at Kaesong just south of the 38th parallel in July. The talks continued over the next two years while the fighting went on.

In order to pressure the communists to negotiate more realistically, a naval bombardment was carried out in the Han River estuary area which was still under enemy control. With

8.5 metre tides Frigates were used and *HMAS Murchison* was among the Frigates chosen for the task. From late 1951 until early 1952 the RAN was reinforced with two destroyers, the aircraft carrier *HMAS Sydney* and three naval air squadrons.

Pressured by US President Harry Truman for additional troops in June 1952 a second Australian battalion, 1RAR, joined 3RAR which was part of the British Commonwealth 28th Brigade. With the brigade now more than half Australian, the British agreed to hand over command to Australia's Brigadier Thomas Daly. As the war continued and casualties mounted, on 21 March 1953, 2RAR was the third Australian battalion to be committed to action in Korea.

Until the differences between the UN and communist leaders on the repatriation of P.O.W.'s, who numbered more than 100,000, could be settled there was no chance of an end to the fighting. The breakthrough came on 6 June 1953 when the communists suddenly agreed to the UN's terms on prisoner repatriation and it appeared the way was clear for the signing of an armistice. However, there was a new problem.

The South Koreans insisted that the Chinese armed forces not be permitted to remain on the Korean Peninsula after the fighting ended. This angered the Chinese and they mounted a powerful offensive against the South Korean 5th and 8th Divisions. In retaliation, South Korean President, Syngman Rhee, ordered that all North Korean prisoners who were refusing repatriation to the North be released. About 25,000 walked out of prison camps and melted into the civilian population.

Rhee also stated that unless the Chinese withdrew completely he would 'go it alone'. The UN leaders were shocked and he was told that he would get no military assistance from the

United States military if he did. Rhee finally agreed to the armistice on certain conditions but the war continued until 27 July when the peace document was signed.

Twenty-one nations had responded to the UN's call to assist South Korea. A total of 17,808 Australians served in the armed forces in Korea and 341 died. North Korea remains a threat sixty years on.

8 Platoon 'B' Coy 1 RTB Kapooka, NSW, Intake 3, 1968.
Photo courtesy Bob Wade

4
VIETNAM - 1965 TO 1972

NOEL WALLIS

Australia's involvement in the Vietnam War began in 1962 when the military decided to send a team of thirty jungle warfare specialists as training advisors to Vietnam. This detachment augmented United States advisory teams who were working with the South Vietnamese Army in the northern provinces engaged in suppressing the Viet Cong insurgency. It was all part of the ongoing cold war great power, global chess game.

In 1964, Australia increased its commitment by dispatching an aviation detachment consisting of six Caribou aircraft and seventy-four men to assist in transport operations. The same year, an engineering civil action team of twelve went to assist in rural development projects. In their turn, they were followed by the first of several surgical teams which were stationed in Long Xuyen Province.

Military involvement increased sharply in1965. Australia offered to send an infantry battalion if both the United States and South Vietnam requested it. Following talks at various levels, a task force was agreed to, composed of an HQ element of the Australian Army Far East, the 1st Battalion Royal Australian Regiment, the 79th Signal Troop and a Logistical Support Company.

Of this 1,400 contingent, approximately 100 were jungle warfare advisers to be used in support of the original detachments. This force was placed under the command of US General Westmoreland, but was used only for defence, patrolling base areas and as a mobile reserve. Arriving early June 1965, it was attached to the United States 173rd Airborne Brigade operating out of Bien Hoa. Restrictions on its sphere of operations were effectively lifted two months later.

On 8 March 1966, the Australian Government announced its intention to increase the size of its contribution to a two battalion force with a special air service squadron plus armour, artillery, engineer, signal, supply, HQ, transport, field ambulance, ordinance and shop units. It appears that low key intergovernmental talks to this effect had been conducted for some time. This commitment brought the number of Australian troops to 4,500. Regulars and National Servicemen of the 6th Battalion RAR arrived at the newly established Australian base at Nui Dat on 14 June1966.

Despite, or perhaps because of, the effectiveness and successes enjoyed by the Australian troops, it became clear that a third battalion was needed. Impending elections in Australia caused the decision to be deferred until after November. The re-elected government promptly offered more troops, the guided missile destroyer HMAS Hobart, eight B-57 Canberra bombers and a diving team.

Trooper N. (Normie) Rowe, South Vietnam, 1969. *AWM EKT/69/DOD1/VN*

HMAS Sydney at anchor in Vietnamese waters unloading troops and equipment. *RAN Historical photo*

Returning to Base, South Vietnam,1967. *Mike Coleridge/AWM Neg. E00454*

Another 1,700 troops were deployed over eight months in late 1967 and early 1968. The 3rd Battalion RAR, with combat and logistical elements, was attached to the 1st Australian Task Force in the III Corps Tactical Zone in December 1967. A tank squadron with its logistical supports arrived in late February and early March 1968 with fifteen operational Centurion tanks. Eleven more tanks were added in September. The No.9 Helicopter Squadron received eight additional helicopters in July, bringing the total to sixteen. A cavalry unit of thirty was added in October 1968. The Australian commitment was now over 8,000.

Across the Tasman, New Zealand had contributed to the Vietnam War effort since 1964 when a small detachment of engineering and surgical personnel were used in civil action projects. Up until December 1967 troop strength was increased slightly and New Zealand's total troop numbers reached only

517 by the end of that year. The troops from both countries were integrated into an ANZAC battalion, and a platoon of New Zealand Special Air Services was integrated with their Australian counterparts. Troops from South Korea and the Philippines were also committed to Vietnam.

The Anzac involvement in Vietnam did not enjoy popular support at home. Agitation for troop withdrawals increased throughout 1968 with public demonstrations continuing well into the following year.

The claim can justifiably be made that the decision to commit National Servicemen to active service by the higher echelons of power was made by May 1965, well before the first intake on June 30 of that year. In other words, the Nashos of the 1960's were conscripted for the purpose of active service.

Of the 64,000 young men called up between 1965 and 1972, 23,000 saw active service in Vietnam. The number eventually made up approximately 50% of the Australian Task Force. There were 210 National Servicemen killed during this conflict with some 1,479 wounded in action. Some Nashos were engaged in training men for active duty and some for the transportation of the dead and wounded flown back to Australia. Others were involved in seeing men off in aircraft bound for Vietnam whilst all the time they were awaiting their own turn to go to foreign soil.

One of the first actions taken by the newly elected Labor Government under Prime Minister Gough Whitlam in December 1972 was to order all Australian troops home from Vietnam. This merely accelerated the process already begun by the previous Liberal Government under William McMahon. National Service had now come to an end.

National Servicemen as well as Regulars had to bear together the incessant criticism of various groups within Australian society on our participation in the war. Their return to these shores was just as ignominious. National Service became a dirty word due to Nashos' involvement in Vietnam. Those activists who abused and vilified the returning troops should have confronted the ones who SENT, not the ones who WENT. The stigma was dealt a death-blow in 1987 with the 'Welcome Home' march, and more so with the permanent Vietnam Memorial in Australia's Capital dedicated in 1992.

Honour and due recognition has been restored to those who were conscripted to serve this country at home and abroad. National Servicemen now have their own memorial in Canberra – The National Service Memorial, which was dedicated on 8 September 2010.

THE MILITARY

When nations are in conflict
It's the military's resolve
To clean up all the troubles
Politicians have failed to solve.

COMMONWEALTH OF AUSTRALIA
DEPARTMENT OF LABOUR AND NATIONAL SERVICE
National Service Acts 1951

N.S.27
VG.CJ

CALL-UP NOTICE

To Noel Douglas BROWN, (Reg'n No. Q. 6482)

9 Stonehaven Street, TOOWOOMBA.

Pursuant to Section 26 of the National Service Acts 1951, you are hereby called-up for service with the Citizen ~~Forces~~ Naval Forces.

You are required to present yourself for service at H.M.A.S. Penguin, Sydney.

on the Twelfth day of July 195 4.

to The Commanding Officer.

It will be essential that you travel on the train leaving Toowoomba at 12.10 a.m. on 11th July, 1954.

You are required to report to Naval R.T.O. at South Brisbane Interstate Station at 10.30 a.m. on 11th July, 1954.

Enclosed is a warrant to cover your journeyto Roma Street Station. On presenting this at the Toowoomba Railway Station Ticket office you will be issued with the necessary ticket for travel free of charge.

Dated this Twenty-fifth day of June 195 4.

District Employment Officer.

NOTE.—If you incur expense for fares, meals or accommodation en route (additional to any provision the District Employment Officer has made for you) essential to enable you to comply with this Notice, you may obtain on arrival at the Training Centre, for completion and submission to the Service authorities concerned, a form of claim for recoupment up to the limits prescribed. If a claim is made, this Notice should be attached thereto.

If you are a member of the Citizen Forces or a Cadet, you should inform your Unit H.Q. of your Call-up as soon as you receive this Notice.

N.S. 27 L.N.S. 2/53.

Govt. Printer, Brisbane.

Call-Up Notice

5
NATIONAL SERVICE IN THE NAVY

VICKI BROWN
WRITTEN ON BEHALF OF MY HUSBAND

In early July 1954 an ominous second *Commonwealth of Australia* letter arrived. The first was a Call-Up about two years earlier that had been deferred owing to the Call-Up-ee being an apprentice.

The mixed-goods train known locally as the 'Midnight Horror' rolled out of the Toowoomba Railway Yard on time on a very cold frosty night with four young Toowoomba men bound for National Service. As the train pulled away from its position in the yards near the Russell Street level crossing they waved farewell from the windows of the last carriage, which was a combined passenger and guard's van.

From Brisbane they travelled to Sydney where their Naval Training Base was located. *HMAS Penguin* is situated in the

Sydney suburb of Balmoral on the Hunters Bay area of Middle Harbour.

On Arrival at *HMAS Penguin* the members of the Intake were allotted to a Class. The following were in Class 10, and some became lifetime friends. Under the charge of Petty Officer S.M. Duturbure, were National Servicemen – A. (Tony) Anderson, P. (Peter) Baglin, Sydney NSW, L. (Laurie) Bailey, Raymond Terrace NSW, A. (Bertie) Bertwhistle, Brisbane Qld, R. (Rex) Betteridge, Sydney NSW, K. Bisset, Brisbane Qld, B. (Brian) Black, Sydney NSW, R. (Roger) Boa, Sydney NSW, J. (John) Bogan, Maitland NSW, G. (Gill) Breitkreutz, Ipswich Qld, G. (Graham) Brett, Sydney NSW, N. (Noel) Brown, Toowoomba Qld, T. (Tom) Budden, Red Hill Brisbane Qld, R. (Rooney) Budsworth, Sydney NSW, M. (Michael) Callen, Sydney NSW, A. (Anthony) Cardile, Brisbane Qld, W. (Warren) Champion, Sydney NSW, K. (Kevin) Clews, Chatswood NSW, A. (Allan) Court, Sydney NSW and N. (Norman) Cummings, Sydney NSW.

Of the 20 in this Class Noel was the oldest, being born in 1933, Johnny Bogan, Mick Callen and Warren Champion were 1934 and the rest born in 1935. They were issued with their necessary Navy uniforms and identity cards for admittance to the Balmoral Naval Depot of which *HMAS Penguin* was a part. The identity cards showed for example: Name - Brown N D, Division - 26, Rating - R/Sto (Recruit Stoker) and Religion C/E.

The days were filled with lots of exercise, including carrying their packs around the oval, precision drill, rowing, swimming, gunnery and indoor classes relating to the workings of Navy ships, and outings to various Sydney places of interest e.g. Taronga Zoo. They were often detailed to Garden Island where Naval Ships are serviced and refurbished. On special Naval

Days such as 'Trafalgar Day', which was a traditional 'Open Day', the National Servicemen participated in events in their dress uniform.

Naval Nasho Noel Brown, 1954. *Photo courtesy (Mrs) V. Brown*

About half-way through the Intake time the National Servicemen were allowed a long weekend leave. Noel flew to Brisbane and came home to Toowoomba. It was Carnival of Flowers weekend.

On return to barracks at *HMAS Penguin* it was announced that there was to be a selection of National Servicemen from the Intake to go to sea. At that time the aircraft carrier *HMAS Vengeance* was the Fleet Training ship. *'Vengeance'* was being deployed to Japan in order to bring back to Australia the RAAF's No.77 Squadron following cessation of the Korean War. It appears that a number of Class 10 members were selected.

HMAS Vengeance in Sydney Harbour. *RAN Historical Photo.*

HMAS Vengeance left Sydney on the 27 October 1954 and had probably already loaded the selected National Servicemen from Melbourne. They were each issued with new identity cards for use on 'Vengeance' and Noel's card, in addition to 'Name and Religion', now read 'Division - Training, Starboard Mess 102, Rating - Stoker, and his Pay No.' They were also issued with an on-board Canteen pass, which identified his name and Mess No. only.

The passage to Japan navigated north, well outside the Barrier Reef and between New Guinea and New Britain. *HMAS Vengeance* passed Manus Island, the Caroline Islands, Guam and the Marianas before entering Japan's Inland Sea to berth at Iwakuni. There they loaded No. 77 Squadron. Some planes were intact whilst much of the loading was in crates. They then moved on to Kure, also in the Inland Sea.

Meteor Jet being loaded onto HMAS Vengeance, 1954.
Photo courtesy (Mrs) V. Brown

While at Kure the National Servicemen were allowed shore leave and they visited all sorts of places that welcomed the Australian Servicemen. Some business cards:- Bar Maxim, Food and Drink at 7 Chome, Naka-Dori, Kure, Tel 2292. This card had a Yen/Dollar Conversion rate. At that time $US5 bought 1800.00 Yen. Another card for the Hotel Fukujuso, 7 Chome, Hondori, Kure Tel.2700, advertised *Turkish Bath, Stand Bar and Dancing.* Another – Welcome to the Restaurant Olympic, Naka-Dori 7, Kure. Tel 2418 - *Beer and Cocktails*. Also a label obviously soaked off a bottle - *Kirin Brewery Company, Limited – Lager Beer*. Last but not least a very plain business card from a short ship's visit to Yokosuka - 'By the electricity' DRAGON TATTOO SHOP No.8 1 Chome, Hinode-Cho, Yokosuka. The discrete results of that visit arrived home in the form of a scroll including 'Noel' on one forearm, and a Geisha girl on the other forearm.

When sailing in to berth at Kure, Hiroshima could be seen in the distance and some from Class 10 took the opportunity to visit the ruins. They returned to *HMAS Vengeance* a very quiet group.

Remains of lone building that survived in the centre of Hiroshima where the Atomic Bomb was dropped on 6 August, 1945.
Photo courtesy (Mrs) V. Brown

Following the short visit to Yokosuka, *HMAS Vengeance* headed south via the Marianas and into a typhoon off the Caroline Islands where the deck of *HMAS Vengeance* was partly awash.

After the typhoon the ship's crew held a Crossing-the-Line ceremony at the 'Royal and Ancient Court of King Neptune 'as *'Vengeance'* crossed the Equator.

'By the grace of Mythology, King of the Waters, Sovereign of the Oceans, Governor and Lord High Admiral of the Bath,

Ruler of All Mermaids, Sea Serpents, Whales, Porpoises, Eels, Crayfish, Crabs, Schnapper, Blackfish, Flathead, Cockroaches and all things living in the Deep. Whereas it pleased us to convene a Court in Her Britannic Majesty's Australian Ship 'Vengeance' at sea on Wednesday 3rd November 1954. Certificate signed – *Neptune Rex.'*

So read the certificate issued to the participants, and in turn this was signed by members of Class 10, and a number of others including Larry Pratt, the later famous race caller.

Back in Queensland waters the Pilot from Caloundra took the Customs people out to the *'Vengeance'*. All ships and personnel are subject to rigorous checks for illegal imports. This was completed before the ship docked in Sydney. The Pilot brought in the mail to Caloundra for posting.

Class 10 Colour Guard, HMAS Penguin, 1954.
Photo courtesy (Mrs) V. Brown

At *HMAS Penguin* on the 3 December 1954, for these Navy National Servicemen the days of their service were almost at an end. They were now well-drilled and experienced sailors. For many there was now an option, they would need to consider continuing in the Royal Australian Navy or returning to civil life, a decision which would affect the rest of their lives. Those who returned to civilian life were bound to the Naval Reserve for the following 5 years and had to report each December. They were issued with a booklet of cards addressed to:- The Secretary, Naval Board, Navy Office, Melbourne, S.C. 1, Vic. They had completed 154 days of continuous training.

For N.S. Noel Brown his *Certificate of Service* in the Royal Australian Naval Reserve (National Service) was received after 11 July 1959. This certificate also incorporated his Certificate of Final Discharge from Naval National Service Training.

In the new millennium there was a Media Release by the Prime Minister, The Hon. John Howard, MP, as follows:- '*To mark the 50th Anniversary of the introduction of National Service in 1951, a new commemorative medal will be created to recognise the service of more than 300,000 National Servicemen between 1951 and 1972.....Of the 325,800 National Servicemen over that 21 year period, 187 gave their lives on active service and some 1500 were wounded.....* 26th April 2001'

(The numbers of those who served and died have since been revised. – Ed.)

National Serviceman Noel Brown applied for the Anniversary of National Service 1951-1972 Medal on 8 August 2001 and in due course received a Statutory Declaration form which he had to sign, have witnessed and return to the Dept. of Defence in Melbourne. He was ill and looked forward to the medal arriving. He passed away on 17 April 2002 and his ashes were buried in the Drayton and Toowoomba Cemetery on 25 April 2002 - Anzac Day.

The medal arrived in the mail on 26 April 2002.

Souvenir of the 1954 Voyage to Japan.

SERVICEMEN'S
NATIONAL
ASSOCIATION
51
72
NAVY · ARMY · AIRFORCE

6
A FLEET AIR ARM NASHO

RUSSELL REA

During World War Two I was in Primary School. At the end of the war there was a great lack of trust between the Western Countries and the Communist Countries. This mistrust came to be known as the Cold War. When the Korean War (1950-1953) was being fought I was in High School. The Cold War had intensified so much the feeling was that another war was inevitable. Being aligned with the West, Australia didn't want to be unprepared if or when this war did eventuate. One of the strategies employed was to have enough trained men (no women) ready to fight. This is why National Service came into being.

The plan was for every male when he reached the age of 18 years to register for National Service. Eventually this was followed by a physical examination and an interview. If you were medically unfit that was it. You were exempt. Unfortunately some 'worked' this part to miss out on service.

On the registration form there was a part that asked for a preference of service and your reasons for nominating Army, Navy or Air Force. I selected Navy because my father had spent all his working life at sea, first in the RN (Royal Navy) then in the Merchant Navy Service. Also my brother, who was 2 years older than I, did Navy National Service and was in the Naval Reserve for several years. I became a sailor. Seeing most (about 95%) were sent to the Army and a few per cent sent to the Air Force I considered myself very fortunate to be in the Navy.

Although the registration age was 18, I was able to defer my entrance to National Service for one year to complete my studies. I discovered that my Intake (Oxley Intake) comprised many university students and apprentices. So as not to compomrise their studies and careers too much our service was split into two halves. We did 3 months (Jan, Feb, Mar) in 1955 and a similar 3 months in 1956 so our service took in the months that would least affect our careers. The rest of the 5 year commitment was spent in the Reserve (non-active). During this 5 year period we were liable to be recalled for service if the need arose.

The day arrived when I had to report to *HMAS Rushcutter* where we were assembled and checked off. Our first sea voyage then occurred across Sydney Harbour from Rushcutters Bay to *HMAS Penguin* at Balmoral. This was to be our home for our basic training where we learnt to be sailors. Another thing we learnt was that we were naval airmen – no choice, this is what you are! This suited me.

Naval Airmen Trainees, HMAS Albatross, 1955. *Photo courtesy R. Rea*

One of the first things was the collection of uniforms. We also were given a name stamp and had to stamp every piece of uniform with our name. Next our civilian clothes were to be bundled up and posted home. This we did except for the underpants as Navy issue was something that was most undesirable.

This intake of 60 recruits consisted of nearly equal parts from New South Wales, Victoria and Queensland. This gave us a chance to make new friends from the other States.

Our training started with basic things like how to salute the Navy way, how to stand, march, recognise calls on the bosun's pipe and to call everybody else Sir. How to look after our uniforms e.g. tying the tally band on our caps, ironing the 7 creases in the bellbottoms, wearing the silk and lanyard properly, how to sling a hammock and get into it, etc. The parade ground was called the Quarter Deck so every time we stepped on the parade ground we had to salute just like on a ship.

Our other training consisted of learning the parts of a ship, how to recognise the ranks especially the Officers (because Officers have to be saluted), compass work, naval watches (e.g. Middle Watch is midnight to 0400 hours), tying knots and other rope work, fire fighting, small arms drill, small boat work, swimming efficiency, PT and team games that had to be played during the first Dog Watch (1600 to 1800 hours).

After 6 weeks our basic training was complete and we were given our first liberty. If it wasn't your duty weekend, liberty started first Dog Watch on Friday and ended at midnight Sunday. So Friday afternoon last thing before liberty was 'needle day'. We were inoculated for this and that and if you were going to have a reaction to the latest needle you had to recover in your own time while on liberty.

The next part of training was to be specific for Naval Airmen so we transferred to *HMAS Albatross* which is near Nowra on the south coast of NSW.

At the time, the Fleet Air Arm had Hawker Sea Furies, Fairey Fireflies and Bristol Sycamore helicopters as the main aircraft. The training consisted of crash and rescue organisation, fire fighting, aircraft handling, flight deck organisation, aircraft parts, flight controls, engines, fuels, pneumatics, meteorology, safety equipment, motor transport organisation, ordnance and photography.

After all this basic training we were integrated into the squadrons. I was sent to Squadron 805 which was a Sea Fury squadron. One of the advantages of being in the Navy was becoming part of the regular service and not being treated differently. Our duties as you can imagine were fairly basic. We swept out hangars, parked and cleaned the planes and sometimes refuelled them. One day I even changed a plane's spark plugs (18 of them).

From *HMAS Albatross* we were transported to Sydney then by train to Melbourne where we embarked on the aircraft carrier, *HMAS Sydney*. From Melbourne we sailed to Fremantle, stayed a week then returned to Melbourne. How exciting it was to see planes taking off then later landing on the deck. There was the usual number of incidences where tail wheels would snap off and bounce along the deck then overboard. The crash barrier stopped some but we had to keep out of the way.

Sea Fury109 after missing the arrester wires. *Photo courtesy R. Rea*

During part of the first Dog Watch we had sport - deck hockey or volley ball. The volley ball court was one of the lift wells. Some activities after the evening meal were movies, tombola or maybe a jazz concert by part of the band.

At Fremantle my mate and I spent our liberty seeing Perth and enjoying ourselves. Whilst on duty in Fremantle I was put over the side with another Nasho and a pot of grey paint to paint the side of the ship. We stood/sat on a small plank and had to loosen the ropes holding the plank and lower it to a new place to paint. Seeing the distance from the flight deck to the wharf was quite considerable we worked very carefully.

On the way back from Fremantle I was fortunate enough to get the Middle Watch (midnight to 0400 hours) and because things were quiet I spent 30 minutes at the helm. Just imagine a 19 year old kid in charge of a 20,000 ton ship and about 1200 men.

HMAS Sydney at sea. *Photo courtesy R.Rea*

Back to the civvies for a while then we had to return to *HMAS Albatross* to continue where we had left off. During the break in training another aircraft carrier, *HMAS Melbourne*, had been delivered. *HMAS Melbourne* became the operational ship and *HMAS Sydney* the training ship. That meant we had rookie pilots on board. We embarked at Jervis Bay and sailed to Hervey

Bay in Queensland. To gain experience the new pilots had a lot of 'touch and goes' and also take-offs without using the booster (catapult). In this case we would be in the cat walks along the port side of the deck and after the plane landed we would run out and push the plane aft so the pilot would have enough deck to take-off. Practice for them and fun for us.

Naval Airman Rea parking a Sea Fury. *Photo courtesy R. Rea*

The ship was off Queensland when our National Service time was up so we had to be off-loaded in Bundaberg. The seas were too rough to use the boats so we were flown off the deck in a Bristol Sycamore helicopter. We had to travel back to Sydney by train and then to *HMAS Penguin* where we finished.

The rest of the 5 year service was inactive. In 1960 I received my discharge papers.

Years later I received recognition of my service, being awarded the Anniversary of National Service 1951-1972 Medal and the Australian Defence Medal.

7
AN RANR NATIONAL SERVICEMAN LOOKS BACK

DEAN DACOSTA EM2 RANR (NS)
STURT TRAINING INTAKE JULY 1955

In my twilight years I often muse over my National Service experiences. I suppose the first big lesson I learnt at the hands of a loud and very rude Leading Seaman was that I was in the Navy now, not in an effing restaurant! This lesson was delivered at *HMAS Lonsdale* at Port Melbourne on our first day in the navy whilst having breakfast prior to travel to *HMAS Cerberus* at Westernport Bay. A group of us were lingering over breakfast as we usually did and in no particular hurry, until the aforementioned rude person blasted us out of our comfort zone and into a waiting bus.

How soon we learned that we were really in the navy and not at home in the comfort of mum's bosom, so to speak. The learning curve from then on was very steep and sometimes painful. Our education included the intricacies of the naval seaman's uniform which involved intriguingly-buttoned trousers, tying the tally band bow on a cap, the correct sequence of collar, lanyard and silk, and ironing seven creases in our bells. We learned how to prepare a comfortable hammock, the joy of rousing from that hammock, firstly to the peculiar bugle strains of 'Wakey Wakey' then to the loud voice of our Class Instructor, a rude but greatly respected Chief Petty Officer Coxswain (rudeness must have been a post-graduate course for ranking NCOs).

We learned to recognise but NOT salute a Chief Petty Officer and to recognise AND salute an officer. A shipmate and I found to our cost that failing to observe the latter was not a good thing, no matter how well intentioned. We were walking (sorry, doubling) from A to B at *Cerberus* when we came across an Officer struggling up the road with a suitcase. We knew he would have to drop the case to return our salute, thereby interrupting his struggle, so we considerately averted our eyes and pretended we did not see him. I am sure he was grateful, but what we didn't know was that a Petty Officer was nearby and he rudely (again that trait) bellowed at us, 'Why didn't you two salute that Officer? And I don't want to know.' The end result of that salutary lesson was some time under punishment in the galley.

There were a couple in our class who by dint of university education in one case and the school of very hard knocks in the other, believed at first that they were above naval discipline and that it was all rubbish anyway. They learned. The fellow who was from the hard knock's school was what we called in those days a 'bodgie', hair cut and all. Covered in tattoos he initially exhibited total arrogance and contempt for his fellow class mates. His big mistake was to extend that contempt to our Class Instructor who had some 20 years service, and had excreted better men than 'a Burke Street Bodgie', he told us. It did not take very long for him to learn that the navy always wins. Bereft of his stovepipe pants, hairdo and black shirt and resplendent in his working 8s or his going ashore uniform, he was just like the rest of us and subject to the same discipline and indignities.

Another lad was just a little slow but a nice bloke. Sadly, he could not march. Rather he 'square-gaited', a style of marching whereby the right leg moved in unison with the right arm and the left likewise. One square-gaiter in a group can cause mayhem and lead to extreme rudeness from the Senior Commissioned Gunner (the God of the Parade Ground) and much doubling around with a .303 rifle at the high port. One member of our class came up with an innovative idea to solve the problem. He obtained a broomstick that was held in the recalcitrant's left hand and in the left hand of the sailor in front of him and the left hand of the sailor behind him. As we marched and swung our left arms in unison, the recalcitrant had no choice but to swing his left arm with the rest of us. The success of this idea depended on him keeping in step which he managed after much practice.

Memories of my very early Nasho days at Flinders Naval Depot are still quite vivid. One memory is the swimming test. We were required to jump into the pool fully clothed but without boots and tread water for a specified period. This sounded like a real doddle to us who had spent most of our lives at the beach. Although the test was taken in the indoor pool, we were not aware that the pool was unheated. Anyone who knows the Westernport Bay area of Victoria in July would be aware (as we were not) that the water temperature, indoors or outdoors, can be VERY low. On leaping into the water, the first sensation was of a severe chest restriction and the inability to breathe or shout for help. Self preservation took over and most of us managed to stay afloat, albeit in agony and gasping for breath and having lost all self confidence in our swimming ability. Those of us who passed the ordeal had this skill recorded and those who didn't were required to attend 'backward swimming' classes – nothing to do with back stroke but rather an ambiguous name only the Navy could dream up to describe poor swimmers.

Religion entered into my next memorable experience. At our first Sunday church parade, there was a call for 'Roman Catholics fall out!' Being a Protestant, I stood fast and was duly marched off with the rest of the Proddies to the church. On our return to our living block, we were amazed to find out that the RCs had been able to miss church and have a bludge instead, because the RC Chaplain was on extended leave. Right we thought, a Saint Paul conversion on the road to Damascus is on the cards for the next Sunday. On cue on the next Sunday, a great mass (so to speak) of recently converted Roman Catholics fell out and, as predicted were gleefully sent back to the living block. However, this time the Navy was ahead of us because the duty watch was there armed with brooms and mops and off we all marched to clean up a dirty area for the duration of the church service. Of course, a mass conversion back to Protestantism occurred on the next Sunday.

Other memories concern our sea-time in the aircraft carrier *HMAS Sydney.* We being electricians, they tried to keep us away from guns but the ship's standing orders demanded that even we had to have some knowledge of the ship's defences. Accordingly, they set us up one day with anti-flash gear and sat us behind a Bofors gun in one of the sponsons. The Gunnery Chief told me to keep the cross hairs on the sight within a circle then blaze away at the balloon target. This I did and the tracers arced upwards in spectacular fashion but not within a bull's roar of the target. 'You stupid bastard, you also have to have the target within the circle' he bellowed. Feeling very hurt, I retired back to our workshop with the shouts of the Chief still in my ears, something about 'bloody Greenies', or 'bloody Nashos', or something. However, back in my electrician's comfort zone, I learned invaluable lessons from an Electrician's Mate who fixed items such as potato peelers and loud speakers by simply taking off the covers, leaving them for a while then coming back and screwing them up again. He didn't touch the electrical components but explained to me that '…all they needed was air'. I have remembered this highly technical explanation all of my life and have put it to good use on many occasions.

Whilst alongside in Garden Island Dockyard waiting for *HMAS Sydney* to be made ready for sea, the Navy sent us out in the corvette, *HMAS Cootamundra,* to see how seasick we could get and to practice boat drill. The first task we all passed with flying colours (again, so to speak). The boat drill in Broken Bay was a bit of a farce with the near sinking of the whaler due to the non-coordination of the blokes lowering the falls. This caused the bow of the whaler to attempt a submarine act because the corvette was still slowly under way. Fortunately, the competent coxswain slipped the 'Robinson's Patent Disengaging Gear' (don't you just love that name?) that freed the boat from the falls but dumped it heavily into the sea. The shock of the dump was surely preferable to battling the sharks in Broken Bay. The 'cruise liner' *HMAS Sydney* certainly looked good when we got back.

RANR(NS) Group, HMAS Cerberus, Westernport Bay, Vic., 1955. (Dean DaCosta Row 2, 3rd from right.) *Photo courtesy D. DaCosta*

We experienced an example of the cruelty and warped sense of humour of the Navy when we cruised around the South Australian coast and into Spencers Gulf. A pipe came over that National Servicemen could go ashore when we sighted Port Lincoln. We should have smelled a rat when a further pipe came over that acceptable rig was Number 8s, that is, working rig. However, we all naively swarmed over the side into some motor cutters and were landed on a beach. 'Port Lincoln is over the other side of the Island', a Leading Seaman said. On racing up a sand hill we did indeed see Port Lincoln – across some five miles of water. We were on an island of course, aptly named 'Goat Island'. The ship's company (Officers especially) were highly amused.

There was a little square-off later when we docked at Adelaide's Outer Harbour and were allowed real shore leave in Adelaide. I am an Adelaide native but I made sure I kept this to myself when I wandered around and waited at bus stops. Because of the uniform and the legendary Adelaide hospitality toward sailors, people would pull up in their cars to give me a lift and offer to show me around their city. I was too polite to refuse.

One of our more unusual tasks whilst *HMAS Sydney* was docked in Port Melbourne, was to set up one of the hangars for an Officers' cocktail party. The aircraft lift was raised to the flight deck and the hole left in the hangar deck was filled with water, a walk bridge set up across it and would you believe, live ducks placed in it to provide 'atmosphere'! The payoff for some of the boys (not me of course) was to relieve some of the boxes of a bottle or two of wine as we carried them into the bar in the hangar.

A less savoury but enlightening occurrence was when we were all ordered to line up for a Sick Berth Attendant to inspect our private parts with a magnifying glass and torch. When we asked why, he simply said he was looking for 'crabs'. Most of us had never heard of that nasty affliction and thankfully our mess deck was clear. Not so lucky the Stokers' mess deck. They became an object of curiosity in the showers because of their shaved nether regions, brightly painted with a violet medical paint! We all learned a thing or two about a species of crab that was different to the ones we saw at the beach.

By the time we went to sea, the great levelling that was the hallmark of National Service had taken place. All of us, the university student, the bodgie, the less-gifted and the rest of us had moulded ourselves into a close knit team. A hurt done to one of us was a hurt to the group, whether during a run ashore, or at sea. The recalcitrant learned to march well enough for us not to miss the Leave train which was the punishment for poor marching at Friday Divisions. The university student made a hero of himself by coaching a number of us to a 'pass level' in our final Electrician's Mate exam at the end of our training.

My time in National Service was one that I have valued all of my life. We gained immeasurable confidence in ourselves and learned many skills, not the least being how to work in a team and to trust and support your team in all manner of difficulties. We also learned the value of discipline, not just for its own sake but for the protection it afforded you, your ship-mates and your ship should the going get rough or dangerous. I believe these life skills are lacking in many young people today. I also believe National Service served us well by teaching us very important lessons in an exciting and adventurous environment. I lament greatly that young people of today are deprived of what

I was thankfully obliged to do. I am eternally grateful for that privilege.

SERVICEMEN'S
NATIONAL
ASSOCIATION
51
72
NAVY · ARMY · AIRFORCE

8
NATIONAL SERVICE IN THE ARMY

NOEL WALLIS

CALLED-UP

In September 1952, I received a letter from the National Service Registration Office informing me that I must register for National Service, as in December I would turn eighteen.

In the 1950's each male who turned eighteen years was called-up for National Service. Not all who registered were automatically drafted into service. Some did not pass the medical whilst others had their service deferred due to educational, work or family reasons.

My medical took place at the army centre in the Brisbane suburb of Annerley, and from what I remember, I had some trouble passing water for the urine test. The Orderly told me to take the bottle outside and keep trying. At last I was successful! I was passed A1 and told to present myself at the Kelvin Grove Barracks on 7 January 1953 at 0800 hours.

Buses were waiting at Kelvin Grove on that day to take us to the 11th National Service Training Battalion at Wacol, south-west of Brisbane. We must have looked a motley lot as we disembarked outside the Administration Building to be 'welcomed' by the Duty Officer, and to be supplied at the QM Store with the necessary uniform and equipment.

Wacol Army Camp,1950's. *Thiel Studio photo*

A National Serviceman was issued with one suit of battle dress, one suit of service dress, greatcoat, hat, 3 pairs of drill trousers, 3 khaki shirts, 2 pairs of boots, leather shoes, canvas shoes, 1 pair of shorts for physical training, braces, belt, jersey, 3 singlets, 3 pairs of underpants, 3 pairs of sox, 2 pairs of pyjamas, 3 towels, boot brush, hairbrush and comb, kit bag and eating utensils. We were required to provide our own shaving gear, toothbrush, etc.

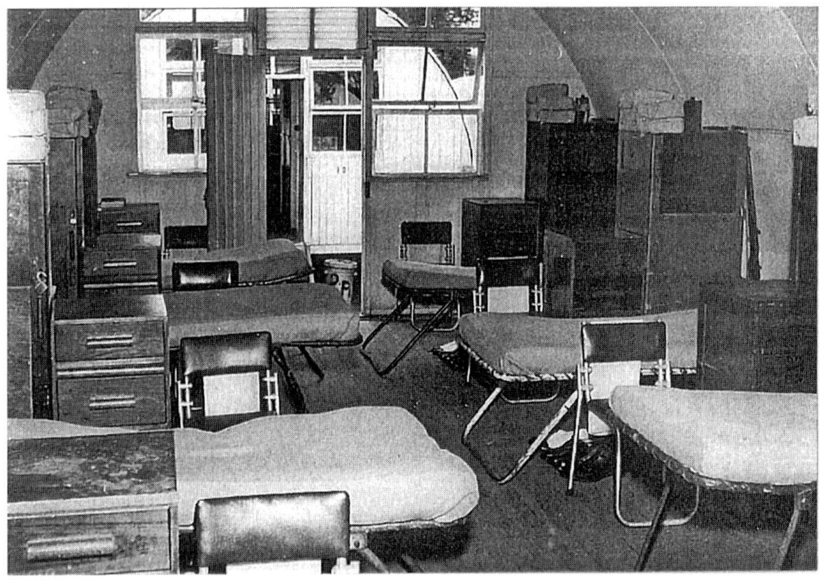

Hut interior, Wacol. *Photo supplied by NASHO NEWS Qld.*

Some of the troops were billeted in dormitory-type huts whilst others occupied long marquees. There were about twenty-four personnel in each tent or hut, and each platoon contained between forty-five and fifty conscripts. In my Intake, there were seven Companies – A, B, C, F and G with four platoons each whilst D and E had six platoons – so there were just over 1500 Nashos in the 1/53 Intake. Over the period 1951-1959, there would have been about 40,500 National Servicemen who passed through Wacol. Add to this all other National Intakes and the total number of young men trained under the National Service Scheme during the 1950's was about 227,000.

Each person had a collapsible iron bed with a comfortable mattress and we were introduced to the art of bed-making 'army style'. Blankets and bed linen had to be carefully folded at the foot of the bed. This was in preparation for tent or hut inspection after breakfast. Alongside of each bed was a small combination wardrobe, drawers and mirror.

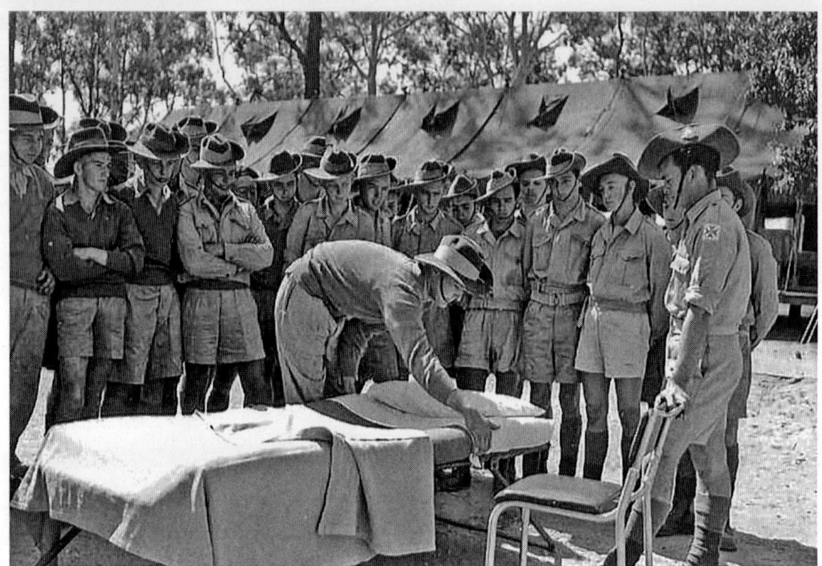

Learning to make a bed the Army way. *Photo supplied by NASHO NEWS Qld.*

The first three Saturday mornings were taken up with injections – two per week. I'm not sure what they were all for but some of those needles hurt! We would line up at the MO tent for this vaccination and strangely, it was normally the big blokes who keeled over, some even before they received the jabs.

One of the early rigours we endured at Wacol was a visit to 'Chicko' – the army barber. He apparently knew only one style (or was instructed to know) and that was SHORT BACK AND SIDES. And how short it was, we must have looked like newly shorn sheep coming out of the barber's shop which was situated in an old army hut. Hanging on the wall he had a ten inches long 'scalp' cut from a 'Bodgie'. Chick Clayton estimated that over 7,000 heads had passed under his scissors at Wacol.

The regular staff of my unit, G Coy 31 Platoon, were decent men. There were Sergeants Hogan and Dick, and Corporals Smith and Revell. Sergeant Dick was a fatherly figure who was meticulous as far as dress and gear were concerned. His own appearance set an example.

The food served from the kitchen was of reasonable quality and there was always plenty of it. Sunday lunch for those who stayed in camp was a treat. How we loved the roast pork and apple sauce. The main complaint we had was all those weevils in our breakfast porridge, and the greasy serving of eggs and bacon. It was suggested by some that the cook sold provisions on the 'black market' but maybe he had a limited budget. One morning on parade after breakfast, an unduly high number of our platoon fainted. We would normally know when a soldier was about to fall – his fixed bayonet would begin to rotate in the air. Often the heat and standing in one spot for a long time would cause this but our Duty Officer was so incensed at the number of his troops to go down that he 'blew the cook up' for serving us bad food.

Ever heard of getting into hot water when there is no hot water? Well, that's what happened at Wacol. The supply of hot water for the kitchen and showers came from the hot water 'donkeys', and they had to be kept alight during the day and early evening then left to die down until the last picket duty from 0400 to 0600 hours. Picket duty was usually on a two-hour roster. We would walk around the perimeter road armed with our side-arm to ward off night 'invaders', check the security of the buildings and generally, try to look occupied. Often those on the last two roster periods would agree to sleep in until 0500 hours and then it was 'all hands on deck' to get the donkeys going. Sometimes because of wet wood, or some other reason, we wouldn't achieve this. We WOULD be in hot water because there was NO hot water and we would cop it from the cook and the troops.

One spot I patronised frequently at Wacol was the Everyman's Hut, a venue for social, recreational and spiritual interaction conducted by Campaigners For Christ. It was similar to the Red Shield Hut in WWII and I found it to be a place of sincere Christian presence in a non-threatening environment and not too religious.

WEAPONS TRAINING

At Wacol most of us looked forward to the out-of-camp excursions we had from time to time. We travelled by chartered bus to the Enoggera Rifle Range or marched to Redbank Rifle Range. Few of us relished the march, or sometimes the jog, to Redbank but once we were there the field experience was a real break from camp.

We learned to fire the .303 at Enoggera and Redbank, and the Owen and Bren guns at Redbank Range. At both places we took our turn in the butts, frequently amongst red-back spiders, where we marked the targets as the bullets whistled overhead, and put the patches over the bullet holes.

During the three months at Wacol, we made only one visit to the grenade range, but that we enough for most of us. The range was an unusual structure of two large log stockade shelters linked by a throwing pit in which there was a low dividing wall. Behind this was the observation shelter where the officer-in-charge stood to watch where we lobbed the grenades and to give instructions. Lining up at the door of the first bunker we received two grenades. Each of us in turn made our way to the throwing pit where one of the regulars was waiting for us.

The instructions were: hold one grenade and give the other to the instructor, remove the pin and throw the missile forward watching where it lands. One then had to squat in the pit until the grenade exploded. If the grenade was accidently dropped in the pit the regular would grab us and throw us over the low wall into the auxiliary pit.

Most of the weapons we used were left-overs from WWII and some of them really showed it. The .303 I received had a pitted barrel and bucked quite a bit when fired. I was always copping it for having a dirty rifle bore on parade. The Bren gun was an accurate weapon that normally rested on a small bi-pod. However, it could also be fired from the hip and instead of recoiling, the gun would pull forward. I found it a very comfortable weapon to use. The Owen gun was an Australian design and was usually fired from a standing position. It tended to lift on the target so one would always need to hold the barrel down. It was a gun of few parts and could be fired almost immediately after being subjected to mud and water.

SPORT

There were various sporting events conducted between the seven battalion companies. Saturday 7 March 1953 was the day of our Battalion Sports at the Battalion Oval. There were track, field and team events and the Northern Command Band provided music during the afternoon.

The boxing tournament was a popular event for many of us. Boxing has long been a prominent and popular sport in all three fighting services. The boxing competition was conducted each Intake at Wacol and for the protection of the personnel competing it was confined to National Servicemen who were amateurs. They needed to be young men of reasonable physical condition, and willing to train in their own time. The finals were refereed by an official referee of the Queensland Boxing and Wrestling Union.

We also had a very capable cricket team which competed in the Northern Command Cricket Association.

The Telegraph Shield was the highlight of parade-ground efficiency. It was the culmination of weeks of training in drill and was referred to almost from the first day of the Intake. The regulars seemed to take the training and competition more seriously than the Nashos. However, we did our best on the big day.

Pte. Noel Wallis, 1953. *Photo courtesy N. Wallis*

SERVICEMEN'S
NATIONAL
ASSOCIATION
51
72
NAVY · ARMY · AIRFORCE

9
A NASHO NCO

HUGH WILLIAMS (CORPORAL)

The day of our medical sticks in my mind as I remember one fellow who was trying to avoid his Call-Up by pretending to be deaf. As he walked out of the MO's office the MO (Medical Officer) dropped a coin on the floor and of course when the fellow turned around he was 'in'. When I was in his office the MO remarked on the fact that I had given my preference to being in the Army. Apparently the majority asked for the Air Force or the Navy.

Eventually the day of reckoning arrived and away we went to Royal Park where they issued us with our equipment. We were led into a large marquee and handed a heap of gear of unknown size. We then swapped amongst ourselves for an outfit as best we could. Only after this exercise were we allowed to go back to the Q store for final adjustments. Finally we ended up with a uniform that fitted. Being Army-wise I knew a few tricks and came out very well-dressed.

I think back to the day I returned to camp after my first Leave. My Mother standing on our front veranda waving goodbye to her soldier son like she had so many times done to my father going off to the War, not knowing if she would ever see him again. I wonder what was going through her mind? Being now a Father and Grandfather I would find it very difficult to see one of my boys going away to an unknown future.

Our training camp at Puckapunyal was about 70 miles north of Melbourne, so we only had two weekend Leaves during the total 98 days. Special buses came up each Sunday to bring visitors. At this stage of my life I was engaged to be married and my Fiancée came to visit me every Sunday without a miss.

Within hours of arriving in camp we were lined up and asked who had military training. On hearing my past service I was immediately put on an NCO refresher course and again got my stripes. This gave me many privileges and I was able to avoid many tedious duties.

One of the jobs I liked was being Orderly Corporal. Being a sadist at heart I enjoyed the job of waking up the Company in the morning. I used to run up the outside of the huts with my bayonet rubbing up and down the corrugated iron making a hell of a racket, then I would return back through the middle of the huts and tip over any beds that were still occupied, tipping the unfortunate Nasho on the floor. The only reason I was not given a thrashing by the boys was the fact of my stripes.

Another trick was if there was an activity I did not want to take part in I would put a clipboard under my arm, look important and walk about looking busy. I was never questioned.

The newly-crowned Queen Elizabeth was due to visit Australia for the first time as the Monarch. A special Guard of Honour had to be trained for her visit to Melbourne. I was chosen and the hard training started. We were trained by an Officer from a British Guards Regiment and we were great. When we eventually marched through the streets of Melbourne the crowds applauded. I don't think I have ever felt so proud. I found a letter amongst my Father's papers that I had written at the time.

Dear Mum and Dad, Thursday

Well at long last it is all over and it was the most wonderful experience that I have had. I have never been so proud of my uniform or Country in my life.

It was beaut to be in such a wonderful thing. The crowd cheered as we marched on and did our drill (which was terrific even if I say so myself). They clapped every drill movement and not only that but the Queen passed not more than 4 feet from me and I saw her as plain as could be. Prince Phillip waved to the boys as he went past. I will tell you all about it when I come home as I will get writer's cramp if I tried to tell you all about it now.

Love Hugh

The only sour note was the return trip to camp. We were taken down in nice clean spacious carriages, but on the return trip we were treated like cattle. We were very disappointed!

The rivalry between the 14th and 15th Battalions was encouraged and every effort was made to be better than our brother Battalion. The food was fair but limited and we were always hungry. So one night we dressed up in full guard uniform and changed their Guard in the dark about 15 minutes earlier than usual and then we cleaned out their kitchens of dozens of trays of apricot pies. We had apricot pie running out our ears by morning as all evidence had to be disposed of. We put the empty trays under the Sergeants' Mess. As we all wore the same uniform it was difficult to tell the difference between the Battalions. Our CO's in their wisdom developed different 'bashes' in our hats. We had a point at the front and the 14th had the square bash, but we managed to get away with it in the dark without detection. There was a hell of a stink about it all but they never found out who did it.

I was able to make a few bob ironing other blokes' shirts and pants as many of these young men did not have a clue. I charged 1/- per shirt and the same for a pair of pants. As I mentioned earlier we only got two Leaves while we were away. We would go down to Melbourne on a Friday night and return on the train on the Sunday afternoon. On our second Leave I decided to take my chances, miss the train and hitchhike back later in the day. Well I just made it as I arrived back at camp only 5 minutes before my Leave Pass ran out. When on Leave the Pucka stripe was a dead giveaway. This was the stripe caused by the chin strap and the sun.

The injections were a curse as they always gave them to us the eve before going on Leave. Some of us were sick while on Leave, a lousy trick. Two other blokes and I did a terrible thing, when this was going on. We pretended that one of us had suffered terribly due to the injections and the other two carried him out of the hut and down past the queue of the waiting men. As you can imagine this caused a major drama, they were dropping like flies. I was lucky not to lose my stripes as while doing this a voice boomed out 'Corporal Williams, you and your mates to the Orderly room'. Fortunately the CO had a sense of humour. He gave us a blast and let us off.

Another trick we pulled involved a fellow in our hut who always managed to return to the hut very late and make a lot of noise getting into bed. We removed his bed and wardrobe and moved all the other beds up to fill the space. When he returned in the dark he would count the beds to find his own. Of course he was to find his bed to be occupied, so recounted again and again. Eventually he started to wake people who were pretending to be in a deep sleep. He was ignored for some time until the lights came on and he was abused by the whole hut (about 35 men). As his bed was missing and it was late at night he spent the night on the floor. He got the message and from then on was always back before Lights Out.

Yet another funny thing comes to mind that took place in the mess hut. We were dished up a meal with dehydrated peas that were like bullets. One fellow decided to flick a pea with his knife at one of his mates. This started a rain of peas as thousands started flying around the hut. We were reprimanded and made to clean it up by the Duty Officer but it was fun while it lasted.

My Company consisted of 60% apprentices and 40% University students and in those days there was a definite distinction between professional people and the trades. These students did not like the idea of being ordered about by the likes of me (I was only a tradesman). One of these fellows came up to me and said, 'Who's ar-- did you lick to become a Corporal?' I was furious as I had worked very hard for my stripes. A couple of days later we went on a 25 mile route march in full gear. We all had our .303 rifles that weighed 9 pounds 4 ounces but the Bren gun was about 27 pounds. Guess who carried the Bren? My friend with the nasty remark.

I was always against 'bastardisation' long before the word was heard of. I did not agree with all that boot polish rubbish and I did all in my power to prevent it happening within my area of command.

An unfortunate accident happened in the Intake previous to ours. It appears a Regular Army Sergeant was looking over the sand bags of the trench when he was hit with the base plug of a grenade. So all our instructors were very strict and all procedures were carried out to the letter. The grenade range was possibly the most dangerous part of training as a lot of the trainees were terrified. One pulled the pin out and then froze while another dropped his after pulling out the pin. The instructor had to stay very calm and in the first case prise the grenade from his hand then throw it. In the second case very calmly pick it up and then throw it.

One of the privileges of being an NCO was the job of using up the surplus ammunition. We would fill up the Bren guns and blaze away. It was good fun. Some of the rifles were very old, mine was dated 1918. I think the bullets went up the barrel sideways, they were so old and worn.

One morning I appeared on parade and had forgotten to shave my upper lip and the Sergeant asked if I was growing a moustache. Of course I had to say, ‘Yes I am’. That was the birth of my moustache which I still have to this day.

I started to have trouble with pains in my legs and I went to the MO for a check-up and it was found that one of my legs was shorter than the other by about ½ inch. The MO asked if I had ever had polio. When I later questioned my Mother I was to find out that I had polio in 1937. She had never told me.

Towards the end of my 98 day stint I was nearly killed by the Artillery. We were out on exercises and on awakening very early to shell-fire, it was found that we had set up camp in the middle of the 25 Pounder Range. We rapidly packed up and got moving in a flash.

Cpl. Hugh Williams, Victorian Scottish Regiment, 1956.
Photo courtesy H. Williams

Our three months' stint was drawing to a close and it would not be long before we were to go home. I had a three months' holiday at the Government's expense and I enjoyed every minute of it. When the last day drew close I was called to the Duty Office and was asked if I would like to enlist in the Regular Army and go to Duntroon. As I was engaged to be married and knew the problems of married life in the Army I declined.

On returning to work I had to go to night school to catch up and also CMF training plus spend time with my girl. A busy time but I was young and fit.

10
MEMORIES OF A RELUCTANT NASHO

PAT O'SULLIVAN

When my Call-Up for National Service arrived it was an unwelcome intrusion into farm life. I was the principal bread-winner on our property that specialised in stud dairy cattle.

We had won two Brisbane Exhibition show milking competitions. The last one was an Australasian record, so we had our honour to defend. Furthermore, if we could win again we could claim the prestigious Courier Mail Trophy. To claim this trophy you had to win it three times.

After discussion and reflection we decided I could take the show cattle team to the Toowoomba Royal Show before the National Service Intake and be back for the Brisbane Ekka.

I had spent two years in the cadets at boarding school and decided that 3 months National Service could not be that much of a hassle.

Like all the National Service recruits from the Darling Downs I travelled by train to Wacol and then by military truck to the camp site. As luck would have it the truck I was in broke down and while we waited for another truck to pick us up I engaged in conversation with a friendly Regular Army Sergeant. I asked his advice about how to handle my new venture and after looking me over he said, 'You're a tall 'handsome' bloke and you will stand out so my advice to you is to stand towards the back of the group and bend your knees. That way you will avoid the attention of the Drill Sergeant.' I can tell you it worked a treat. I felt morally obliged to pass this advice on to my fellow tent mates, which I did two days before the end of camp.

Marquee accommodation, Wacol. *Thiel Studio photo*

We arrived in camp late at night and were issued with army clothes – one size fits all. I pitied the little blokes who were issued with XXOS trousers. (They could swap them the next day.) Generally, we Nashos adapted well to our new life and appropriate nicknames were soon given to some of our fellow Nashos.

Pte. P. O'Sullivan (2nd from left) Wacol, 1953. *Photo courtesy P. O'Sullivan*

'Bodgie' had lots of hair and was very proud of it. He had to have two haircuts in one day. The second haircut was supervised by the Sergeant and the poor fellow was unrecognisable afterwards.

'Gabby' found it hard to stop talking and reminded us of Gabby Horan of radio fame.

'Shoulders' as the name implies, had broad shoulders. He arrived in camp in an intoxicated state and wore the wrath of the Regular Army Corporal for some time.

'Incredible Hulk' - a huge bulk of young man who gave his fellow tent Nashos a rough time. He fancied himself as a boxer and told everyone who would listen that he was about to become the Heavyweight Champion of the whole camp. After being belted around the ring in his first bout by an opponent several stone lighter, he became much more subdued and polite to his fellow Nashos.

Generally speaking, we were a happy, well adjusted lot who helped one another in times of need but delighted in cutting skites down to size. The discipline in camp was necessarily strict but mostly fair. We learnt to respect authority and our fellow Nashos. We accepted that we had to take our turn in doing the 'not so glamorous' jobs.

Personally, I enjoyed the opportunity to engage in different sports, particularly basketball and boxing. I had some success at boxing. Leave enabled a country bloke to experience some big city nightlife.

When camp ended I was able to take our show team to the Ekka. We won the milking competition, setting another milking record and claiming the Courier Mail Trophy.

The country Nashos were not obliged to attend CMF but we did two fortnight camps at Greenbank.

On reflection I was not concerned about the possibility of overseas service and did not give much thought to it. I did not realise at the time the great benefits that National Service afforded me. It was a great influence for good in my later life.

I was not a very active member of the National Servicemen's Association until approached to make horse rugs for our race meeting by a fellow Nasho.

I accepted the position of Secretary on the condition that my wife was Assistant Secretary (she does all the work). I have always prided myself as being good at delegating!

A number of wives of Nashos now fill various supporting roles and bring a caring and insightful atmosphere to our meetings and functions.

11 Battalion Parade, 1953. *Thiel Studio photo*

SERVICEMEN'S
NATIONAL
ASSOCIATION
51
72
NAVY · ARMY · AIRFORCE

11
TRAINING ARMY NATIONAL SERVICEMEN

CARL BLUME (SGT)

My transfer from Southern Command Workshops to the Royal Australian Electrical & Mechanical Engineering 32 Platoon, George Company, 11 National Service Training Battalion in 1954, was a massive shock to my system. It reminded me of my initial recruit training at the Enoggera Training Battalion. There we lived in comfortable hut accommodation. However, at Wacol we had large marquees with trainees at one end and staff at the other end.

This initiation, I believe, made it easier for me to understand the attitudes and concerns of the young fellows who arrived by bus at the start of each Intake.

As each bus arrived and they disembarked, the assortment of clothing and footwear being worn was amazing. Everything from swim shorts and thongs to shirts, ties and suits were worn.

The first week was enough to stress the strongest-willed young person

Line up, strip for a medical check, receive inoculations for tetanus, TB, etc, then line up and march to the Mess hall for lunch. Line up again, march to the Company Q Store for bedding and work clothes. March to the marquee which was to be their home for the basic training period. Here, they were able to make a choice of stretcher and position if they were quick.

Then lessons began on making beds 'Army' style, the location of hygiene facilities and instructions on what the Army expected. This included short back and sides haircuts, daily shaving, etc. Some of the lads had never seen a razor in their lives. Line up again and march to the barber. The result was shorn heads that would have done a shearer proud.

Time for a shower, community-style, change into work gear then line up and march to the Mess for 5 pm tea. Lights out at 10 pm.

Next day, 6 am Reveille set the start of the daily time schedule which was to continue for the next three months.

Line up, this time for the Battalion Q Store (a series of Marquees with long benches and piles of clothing, hats, boots, etc.) for the issue of dress uniforms. Under such a system it was amazing how smart the trainees turned out for major parades, especially for Leave, the most important of all.

The issue of equipment continued: belt, webbing, gaiters and so on. They then had lessons on cleaning (to be done daily) and assembling for inspections at 8 am daily, Monday to Saturday.

Achieving the expected standard of accommodation could become monotonous for the trainees so for later Intakes we devised a 1 to 3 points system. Trainees who received a certain number of points were rewarded with an extra Leave period that week.

The system worked perfectly. The trainees had the opportunity to gain extra Leave and 22 Platoon continuously won the weekly competition. Believe it or not the prize was six (6) bags of cement. Saturday morning was then spent laying new paths to and from 22 Platoon's two huts. A great help when it rained.

The first Intake of 1955 started with a reorganisation of some Battalion Units. 'E' Easy Company became the Engineering Company. Platoons 19, 20 and 21 were Engineers, 22 and 23 R.A.E.M.E., with 24 Signals. The advantage was that we moved to huts which were more comfortable and easier to maintain.

Today I feel a little sorry for some of the lads who didn't reach the standard to gain points for extra Leave. With 18 trainees per hut and competition so keen I believe a more understanding approach by the regular army staff would have been appreciated by some of the trainees.

I believe most trainees strived hard at everything that was required of them. However, there were times when a little discipline was required. 'YOU WILL FIX BAYONET – DUMMIES', was a penalty imposed to be performed after the day's work was completed. This became a favourite saying the lads copied.

Towards the end of the last Intake for 1956, I was Duty Platoon Commander of 'E' Company and was working late at night in the Platoon office when a group of trainees gathered outside. I sensed something was going on. A brainwave occurred. I rang Company HQ and came up with the excuse that the Colonel was on the prowl and was on his way to 'E' Company. I hightailed it over to HQ. Next morning I learnt that the Nasho NCOs had a 'dipping' under the shower. Luck saved them from a 'ducking'.

22 Platoon, 'E' Coy, 11 NST Battalion, April-July 1956 Intake. (Sgt. Blume Row 2, 5th from left.) *Thiel Studio photo*

Over the time I was with 22 Platoon Intakes, I never ceased to be amazed at the skills and abilities of the young people who passed through. Those youngsters would never know or realise the pride we, the regular army staff, had in the lads when they completed their training. In a short time such was the difference between how they arrived and the appearance, discipline and comradeship shown by the trainees on completion of their training.

I would like to congratulate all those young men who passed through 22 Platoon. These thoughts were also expressed by Sgt/ Major Les Steele whom I met on his retirement from the army.

11 Bn. Journal 2/56 Intake

12
RECOLLECTIONS OF AN AIR FORCE 'BOD'

BILL SANDERSON

I was conscripted into National Service Training Unit 14, RAAF Base Amberley, from July to December 1955, the second-last Intake before the Air Force scheme was abandoned.

Nothing about my service was either hard or dangerous except for one occasion when I was on a firing mound next to another ACR (Aircraftsman Recruit) whose Thompson sub-machine gun had a triple feed and sprayed projectiles and bits of cartridge case all over the place out of the exploding breech.

It's a mystery how anybody in battle ever hit anything with a Tommy gun. The short-barrelled .45 calibre weapon had a nasty habit of rising upwards in a right hand arc when fired. I was rarely able to hit a Man Two target at 20 paces but then I flunked Bren gun also, so I may not have been typical.

When called up for National Service, I applied for the RAAF because Air Force 'bods' got their service over and done within one six-months stint, compared to Army types who did three months and then weekly parades and annual camps for two years. I wasn't very happy being dropped into the frame. Not that I was opposed to 'duty to God and the Queen' but because I had a good job and a promising career ahead of me.

My employer made up the difference between the pittance paid to Nashos and my working wage over the entire six months. You would go a day's march to find such an employer these days.

I was trained in aerodrome defence after failing to qualify for pilot training at Archerfield (something about having no sense of balance and chronic vertigo).

'Aerodrome defence' involved a lot of parade ground drill, bush bashing, weapons training (Lee Enfield, Bren, Thompson and Mills bomb) and watching the odd World War 2 training film on subjects such as field camouflage. The films were designed for European conditions and therefore useless to a soldier who might have to fight in tropical jungles.

It's curious what one remembers later in life. I still remember the serial number, E33162, of my Lee Enfield .303 rifle, a 1914 model with a heavily scarred stock and other wooden parts. I used to wonder if it had seen service in Flanders, North Africa or on the Kokoda track and what happened to its previous owners. The .303 was heavy and cumbersome and slow in operation but lethal. We were told it could kill at a mile's distance.

There was a lot of what seemed to me at the time, to be pointless regimentation and discipline. It took a few more years of growing up for me to realise that the object of services discipline is to get people to do what they are told, instantly and unquestioningly, in battle. The instruction in discipline, including self-discipline and co-operation with others, has done me no harm and, indeed, a great deal of good throughout my life.

'Conshie' was the derogatory name given to Nashos who took their service very, very seriously. A 'conshie' was the bloke who, on a unit exercise to run, walk, jog or crawl five miles in under an hour in full battledress, was back at base in 45 minutes – 30 minutes before the rest of us. A 'conshie' was the bloke who, although not a sycophant, was first to stick up his hand to volunteer for some not highly regarded assignment. Everybody professed to dislike 'conshies', but I think we all respected them, privately, for having more of the 'the right stuff' than the rest of us. They are probably amongst those blokes who charge gun emplacements to save their mates.

A revamped National Service scheme would not be a bad idea in these unfortunate times of high unemployment and directionless youth. Of course, this proposition would meet with the strident opposition of do-gooders, civil libertarians, misguided pacifists and others who are out of touch with the real world.

(One opposing view is that the armed services should not be required to solve unemployment and social problems. – Ed.)

In my last month of National Service I was 'excused duties' to help write and edit our Intake's souvenir magazine for which I wrote a rather pretentious editorial concluding that Australia should always 'Be Prepared'. I have recently re-read that editorial and disregarding its immaturity, still think that 'Be Prepared' is a good motto for Australia's defence policy.

I salute all those Australians who have had bullets, cannon shells and other ordinance fired at them in defence of our country. They are the salt of the earth.

Air Force National Servicemen march, Brisbane, 1952.
Photo supplied by NASHO NEWS Qld.

Flypast at Amberley RAAF Base, June 1952. *Photo supplied by NASHO NEWS Qld*

13
NASHOS
IN THE UNKNOWN WARS

BORNEO

The first combat service by National Servicemen was not in Vietnam but Borneo. Between 1963 and 1966 Indonesia and Australia were involved in an undeclared war when President Sukarno launched Konfrontasi (Confrontation) against the newly-formed Malaysian Federation. Two of the 212 Nashos who died on active service were lost in Borneo. Private Michael O'Dea recalls his service in this article and photo from the Department of Veteran Affairs' website, 'Australians at War':

Private Michael O'Dea was called up for National Service in 1965 but unlike many of his colleagues he didn't go to Vietnam. Instead, in 1966 he went to Borneo where Indonesian guerrillas were infiltrating.

He recalls there were about 80 in the second Intake of National Servicemen.

'We were divided up into two groups, 30 going to Borneo and the other 50 to South Vietnam. Several of the group who went to Vietnam were killed or wounded in battles like Long Tan. We will not forget those fellows, who we trained with, lived, joked, played football and went on Leave with. We also knew their families.

The job in Borneo was different to that facing the troops in Vietnam.

We were replacements who arrived there at the end of May, early June. The date I remember as I thought that I would not be able to have my 21st birthday at home. We flew to Malaysia. From Terandak Barracks, Malaysia, we sailed for Kuching, arriving 6 June and joined 4RAR in the Bau area, which was considered the key to Kuching, the capital, just 50 km away.

I was assigned as a rifleman to 8 Section, 6 Platoon, B Company, which was at the forward Company base, Stass, protecting the Stass Kampong 2000 metres from the border with Indonesia. My section did patrols along the Gunong Raya and around Stass base to the border of Indonesia.

My section was under strength because of sickness and injury so we joined up with another section to make only seven or nine men on a patrol where there should have been 20 men in two sections. About half way through the tour of duty I took over on the machine gun when the regular gunner was taken ill.'

The 'Konfrontasi' or confrontation by Indonesia against Malaysia was due to President Sukarno's objection to the merger of the Federation of Malaya with Singapore, Brunei, British North Borneo (now Sabah) and Sarawak. Active objections had started in April 1963 when Indonesians crossed the border at Tebedu close to Kuching in Sarawak. Malayan forces were small in number and all British troops serving in Borneo were in Brunei, having helped to put down the Brunei revolt the previous year.

The British Commander-in-Chief, Major General Walter Walker (Director of Borneo Operations - DOBOPS), had the task of defeating the Indonesian aggression on a 1600 km frontier. Initially, ill-trained and poorly-armed Indonesian border terrorists threatened the border. Then, in 1964 the Indonesian Government strengthened the forces with regulars, and by 1965-66 had trebled their regular garrisons in the Kalimantan/Sarawak area and were operating at almost Army divisional strength.

The Commonwealth forces were dealing with the regular Indonesian Army in an undeclared war. The Australian Government agreed to commit Australian troops to assist the Malaysian and British forces which formed part of the British 28th Commonwealth Brigade, and in April 1965 3RAR moved from its base at Terandak in Malaysia to Sarawak and stayed until August of that year. In April 1966 4RAR moved to the same area.

Borneo was not Vietnam. In 1966 the thirty Nashos who were selected to go to 4RAR were the first National Servicemen to serve in operations. They had completed their training at Ingleburn and the Jungle Training Course at Canungra in Queensland and went as replacements for an under strength regular battalion, 4RAR, which was already overseas, having gone to Malaya in April and from there relieved 1/10 Gurkhas in the Bau District in Sarawak.

The aim of the whole military operation was to identify and defeat Indonesian aggression, or confrontation, and prevent the conflict from escalating into open war similar to that of South Vietnam. Neither side ever publicly admitted that these operations were taking place. The codename 'Operation Claret' was specific to cross-border operations and very few senior offices (on a need-to-know basis) and the troops involved (the latter being sworn to secrecy) had any knowledge of these operations. It was not until 1989 that information was downgraded from Top Secret and details were in the public domain as published in *SAS Phantoms of the Jungle* by David Homer (Allen and Unwin 1989 & 1991). In 1996 further information was released and soldiers could tell their wives and families some of what had gone on.

Private M. O'Dea, Borneo, 1966. *Photo supplied by NASHO NEWS Qld.*

Initial penetrations were limited to 5000 yards (4572m) but later his range could be, and often was, increased to 20,000 yards (18.288m) for specific tasking. The aim was purely to keep the Indonesians on the defensive by forming a 'cordon sanitaire' on the Indonesian side of the border. The potential political ramifications were in the extreme, hence the need for absolute secrecy. On no account were injured or dead soldiers allowed to fall into enemy hands. Neither side admitted incursions into the other's territory.

'Claret' operations were suspended on 28 May 1966 and on 3 June, Indonesian Radio announced the end of the confrontation.

Australian patrols continued almost without a break and public records show that on 13 June shots were fired south of Stass, and on 15 June two contacts were made with the enemy: the first with two enemy believed wounded; the second, four believed killed and two Australians wounded.

Private V.H. Richards died five days later in Singapore of his wounds. Lieutenant R.G. Curtis of 9 Platoon, C Company was awarded the Military Cross for his cool leadership, bravery, judgement and determination in leading nine men to block the withdrawal of an enemy party during this action, and Corporal R.R. Anderson was awarded the Military Medal.

Helicopters supplied the needs of Mick O'Dea and his mates in B Company; the huge Bristol Belvedere turbine-engined craft had the capacity to carry 19 troops, or 12 stretchers, or 6000 lbs (2721 kg) freight (fresh rations, defence stores, and the 105 Pack Howitzer slung beneath it). The light 2-3 person Bell Sioux helicopters with external racks for freight or stretchers were used for command and control of the large battalion areas.

Number 8 Section, 6 Platoon B Company patrolled the border as a section, took part in larger sweeps and did not escape the tedious but necessary tasks of clearing fields of fire for the company base at Stass against the continually growing primary jungle on the ridges, lalang grass and secondary growth that grew to a height of three and a half metres in the valley floor.

Operational service in Borneo ceased on 11 August 1966 and the confrontation ended officially on 16 August with the signing of the accords in Jakarta by Razak and Malik, and Sukarno surprisingly also receiving the visiting Malaysian delegation. 4RAR was relieved in early September by 3 Battalion Royal Malay Regiment.

The British General Service Medal (GSM) with the clasp, Borneo, was issued to those who saw special service between the dates of 24 December 1962 and 11 August 1966, in Sarawak.

Australian officers and other ranks saw service there during April-August 1965 (3RAR); April-September 1966 (4RAR). 102 Field Battery moved to Borneo in May 1965 until they were relieved in late July 1965. 104 Field Battery served from September 1965 to January 1966. The Australian SAS 1 and 2 Squadrons saw service there in 1965 and 1966. Units of the Royal Australian Engineers 1st and 7th Field Squadrons and 21st/22nd in the Bau-Stass area were primarily involved with road building and built an airstrip at the junction of the Kaumut and Milian Rivers in Sabah.

Australian casualties during the Indonesian confrontation were four killed in action (two Regulars and two Nashos), one died of wounds, two drowned on operations and one died of sickness. Four were killed accidentally and two committed suicide. Non-fatal casualties were seven wounded in action, one accidentally wounded in action, one of battle exhaustion, and 11 accidentally injured. British casualties were nine killed and 44 wounded, and the Gurkhas lost 40 killed and 83 wounded. Indonesians killed numbered 2000.

'Looking back, I never felt the same as those who went to Vietnam', Private O'Dea wrote. 'We were never acknowledged the same and it took years before even they were acknowledged publicly. Vietnam was an undeclared war, to me Borneo seemed even less.'

The material for this article on Borneo was based on a story written by Tony James and supplied by Michael O'Dea, both of New South Wales.

MALAYA

George Lovett served as a Nasho from September 1971 until March 1973 and saw service with 6RAR which formed the Australian component of the 28 ANZUK Brigade based in Tendaken, near Kuala Lumpur. ANZUK was a tripartite force formed by Australia, New Zealand and the United Kingdom to defend the Asian Pacific region after the UK withdrew forces from the east of Suez in the early 1970's.

George wrote: 'In terms of the number of Nashos involved it would be approximately 50 with 6RAR and possibly the same with 1RAR. Our group of 12 joined 6RAR as reinforcements in May 1972. We spent 11 months on tour. There were about three reinforcement rotations a year with about 12 Nashos in each rotation. Many other Nashos also served with 6RAR, however, there is a component of Nashos who rotated from Singapore into what is known as Rifle Company Butterworth.

It was established in 1973 to provide a protective and quick-reaction force for RAAF Base Butterworth during a resurgence of the Communist insurgency in Malaysia. The RAAF presence required the protection of the RCB force on a twenty-four hour continual basis because there was a real threat and the possibility of attack or incursion by forces of the Communist terrorists whose leader, Chin Peng, fought a long lasting war against the Malaysian Government and Malaysian Armed Forces in order to destabilise and overthrow the Government. The Malaysian Air Force was on active service and was fighting a real war within its own country and on the border with Thailand. The BAB was subject to varying levels of alert. Many of these increased levels of alert were known as 'Red Letter Days' indicating expected CT activity. On such days the entire BAB would go into total lock down, extra air defence measures would be deployed, RCB security patrols were increased, RCB would man fighting pits at the southern and northern ends of the runway, roadblocks and vehicle check points were set up and weapons were in the action condition.

When the Whitlam Government came to power in December 1972 it fulfilled its election promise to abolish National Service. National Servicemen were given a choice to be discharged immediately using the pretext of 'exceptional hardship' or to finish their two year obligation. We could catch the next plane back to Australia if we wished. A few of us stayed with 6RAR to finish our terms as Nashos. In January 1973 D Coy 6RAR rotated to Rifle Company Butterworth (RCB) where we operated under rules of engagement and carried live ammunition. We were possibly the last Nashos to serve on an overseas posting....'

RAAF Base Butterworth was handed to the Royal Malaysian Air Force in 1988 and insurgency officially ended in 1989.

Reprinted from the NASHO NEWS (Qld) May 2012 edition.

14
LOOKING BACK ON LONG TAN

BRIAN CUNNINGHAM

August 1966: The ABC newsreader's solemn voice emanated with perfect enunciation from the radio's speaker, 'Seventeen Australian soldiers were killed on Thursday afternoon in a fierce battle fought in a rubber plantation in South Vietnam. The 17 deceased soldiers were all members of Delta Company, Sixth Battalion, Royal Australian Regiment.'

Mum and I were alone in the kitchen, finishing our breakfast. Both of us sat numbed as if unable to accept the enormity of the disaster. I could see my own shock mirrored on Mum's face, which was rapidly draining of colour as the news reader continued with the details of his announcement.

'Approximately one hundred soldiers from Sixth Battalion were on a routine patrol in the Long Tan rubber plantation five kilometres to the east of the Australian base at Nui Dat. The soldiers encountered, fought and defeated an estimated 2500 Vietcong guerrillas and North Vietnamese Army soldiers who were getting ready to attack the still unprepared defences of the new Australian base at Nui Dat. Next of kin of those killed have been notified. The following is a list of names of the 17 soldiers who died in the battle...'

Our shock deepened as we heard Dennis McCormack's name read from the list.

Sadly, on August 27, 1966, a member of the Royal Australian Armoured Corps died in hospital from wounds he received at Long Tan, increasing the total number of soldiers killed in the battle to 18.

Dennis McCormack had lived about 200 metres up the road from me in the outlying Brisbane suburb of Stafford. We had gone to the same school, Padua College, where he had been a couple of grades ahead of me. Although he was not one of my close mates, he was one of the neighbourhood kids who was always around as I was growing up. It had been a matter of some importance and communal pride in our street when Dennis was called-up for National Service, becoming the only Nasho most of us knew. The first time he came home on leave, wearing his Aussie soldier's slouch hat, he was given instant and sincere respect from all who saw him.

The Battle of Long Tan was fought in torrential rain late in the afternoon and into the night of August 18, 1966. About two weeks later, Dennis's body was returned home, enabling his funeral to be held. On the day of the funeral, September 5, 1966, I took leave from my work as a teller at the Commonwealth Bank to join with the other mourners in paying our last respects. The kids from our old school formed a guard of honour as the hearse carrying the flag-draped coffin left the Little Flower Church grounds on its way to the Pinnaroo Lawn Cemetery.

I was 18 years old when Dennis was killed. His death was the first time the Vietnam War had touched me personally.

While I was growing up, I was absolutely awed when first learning about the legendary, original ANZACS fighting Johnny Turk on the cliffs at Gallipoli. I was further amazed when hearing the stories of later battles fought by Diggers against the murderous Hun in the trenches on the Western Front in WWI.

Then I was equally inspired by the tales of the battles fought against the cruel Nazis in WWII by the next generation of Diggers in the deserts of North Africa. To top it off, there were stories of heroic Diggers fighting the fanatical Sons of Nippon in the jungles of New Guinea and numerous other Pacific Islands.

All of those stories of glorious deeds helped to shape my perception of what war was like. So, naturally, I felt an enormous sense of pride for Dennis's sacrifice and was especially moved when the soldiers in the honour guard fired their salute to him as his coffin was slowly lowered into the grave.

Instead of Dennis's death discouraging me from ever wanting to go to Vietnam, I found I could hardly wait for my 20th birthday to arrive so I could register to be called-up for National Service and get my chance to follow in the footsteps of the Diggers from bygone eras. As it turned out, I didn't wait that long, instead, volunteering for National Service when I was 18 years old.

A few weeks after the battle, the South Vietnamese Government decided to award the South Vietnam Cross of Gallantry to all the Diggers who had taken part in the Battle of Long Tan. However, the Australian Government forbade the acceptance of the foreign award. The now-embarrassed South Vietnamese officials were forced to produce alternative awards for the men. On the nominated day, the Diggers assembled on parade at Nui Dat to receive their awards, not medals but wooden cigar boxes for the officers, cigarette cases for the non-commissioned officers and dolls dressed in the national costume for women – *the ao dai* – for the other ranks.

Two years later, my platoon was on a patrol in Long Tan, staying overnight at the site of the battle. We harboured-up near the base of the feature called Nui Dat 2. It was not difficult to conjure up the image of the enemy commanders controlling their 2500 troops from that very spot in their fight against the 108 Diggers from D Coy, 6RAR.

The rubber plantation we were harboured-up in was now disused and overgrown with weeds. Even so, we could see many old craters that had been blasted into the ground two years earlier by the artillery rounds fired from Nui Dat. The scene of the battle covered an area about the size of two football fields. Large gaps existed in the long rows of rubber trees. Every rubber tree was still scarred from bullets and shrapnel.

The patrol in the site of the Battle of Long Tan was something of a pilgrimage for me. I had been looking forward to going there since first arriving in Vietnam to quietly remember my old boyhood mate, Dennis MCormack. Dennis's mum had been sending me *Man* and *Pix* magazines on a regular basis. In return, I sent her a doll wearing an *ao dai* outfit, the national costume worn by Vietnamese girls and women. At the time I was unaware that the Diggers who survived the battle had been presented with the same dolls by the South Vietnamese Government.

Long Tan wounded, Vietnam, 1966.
Photo supplied by NASHO NEWS Qld.

It was a deeply spiritual experience for me to be sitting at the place where 18 Diggers, including Dennis, had been killed, and a further 21 Diggers had been wounded. Buried in shallow graves in the ground around us were the bodies of about 250 enemy soldiers.

Coincidentally, there were 18 Diggers in our patrol that day, the same number that was killed in the battle.

In August 1969, three years after the battle, when 6RAR was on its second tour in Vietnam, the Diggers in D Coy returned to Long Tan and placed a large concrete cross to commemorate the supreme sacrifice made by those who had died in the Battle of Long Tan.

Reprinted with kind permission from Queensland RSL NEWS.

HE DIED IN VIETNAM

I looked at the body lying there
The suntanned face, the short blonde hair
Ten minutes ago he was feeling fine
Nine minutes ago he stepped on a mine.

He was a good example of an Australian man
So what was he doing in Viet Nam?
He was doing his duty, he'd signed on the line
And happened to be there on this day in time.

He'll go home now to his friends and kin
And they'll join us grieving and mourning for him
There's no hero's welcome for this young man
Because he died in Viet Nam.

How much must we pay for doing our job?
Why did we come home and face a mob?
There's no hero's welcome for you young man
Because you served in Viet Nam.

Bob Lange

15
A NASHO IN PAPUA NEW GUINEA

PETER WEDGWOOD (SGT)

In 1962 I completed twelve years of schooling and took up a secondary school Science Teaching Scholarship. Because of a shortage of teachers at the time this was a special 'accelerated' course, which meant I spent 1963 at the University of Queensland studying the basics (Chemistry, Physics, Applied and Pure Mathematics) and 1964 learning my craft at the Kelvin Grove Teachers College. At the beginning of 1965 they let me loose on the unsuspecting students at Biloela State High School. It was the first time I had ever been away from home. Later in the year I was transferred to Sandgate State High School and moved back in with my parents and sister at West End in Brisbane.

At some stage during this time (and I really can't remember when) my marble was drawn from the barrel in Canberra and I was informed that I would be joining the Australian Army at the beginning of 1966. I was not overly concerned by this. My father, who had been a Warrant Officer (WO2) in the Signal Corps in WWII, was extremely pleased. He thought it would be a wonderful opportunity for me to get away from the family and learn to stand on my own two feet.

In due course I underwent the compulsory medical. The doctor observed what he considered were my flat feet. He thought about this for a few minutes then asked, 'What is your occupation?' When I replied, 'Teacher Sir', he commented, 'then you are used to standing on your feet all day', and ticked the appropriate box. So now I was really 'in'. On the appointed day I boarded a chartered flight to Sydney and from there ended up at Singleton for basic training.

There are a number of published accounts of the shock that recruits faced in these first weeks of basic training. I became a number in 9 Platoon, B Company. Like all other recruits I learnt the basics and my days were filled with PT, map reading, obstacle courses, rifle firing, grenade throwing, bayonet practice and of course DRILL. Our nights were taken up with polishing boots, preparing our uniforms and rifle maintenance. We had been issued with brand new SLR's and they came encased in thick grease. It was our task to remove all the grease and get them into pristine condition before we could even attempt to fire them. This took many hours. While at Sandgate High I had been instructing a fencing team in the intricacies of using a sabre, so my fitness level and hand/eye co-ordination were good. A plus for all the physical activity.

After the first few weeks we were allowed Leave and I returned to Brisbane to collect my beloved Mini Minor as we were now allowed our own transport. This gave me and some of my Nasho mates a new-found freedom

At the conclusion of recruit training I applied to join the Signal Corps, following in my father's footsteps. I was accepted and transferred to Parramatta for further testing to ascertain which section I would be best suited for. While at Parramatta I celebrated my 21st birthday. There was no fanfare, no receiving of the 'Key of the Door', just a quite 'legal' drink in the Mess.

In March 1966 Prime Minister Holt had decided that Nashos could be required to serve in Vietnam. By April whilst I was at Parramatta the army was looking to fast-track electronic technicians within the Signal Corps so they could serve there, maintaining and repairing wireless equipment. I was selected to do the 'Tech Elec' course, which had previously been a 2 year course, but was now accelerated to 6 months. (Here we go again – another accelerated course.) This might have been because of my qualifications with first year Physics from UQ. Whatever it was I found myself moving to Belcombe on the Mornington Peninsula.

Belcombe in winter has to be experienced to be believed. The wind comes straight off the Southern Ocean and is bitterly cold. The showers were not very warm and in virtually outdoor facilities. You would have to chase the water around just to stay wet. For a young man from Queensland it was quite a shock. I survived until about half way through the Course and I am eternally grateful for what I learnt. It meant for many years I was able to repair all sorts of electronic equipment around the house.

One day I was called to the CO's office. What could be in store? He said, 'You are a qualified teacher aren't you?' 'Yes sir'. 'Then you are being transferred to the Education Corps. You have an instant promotion to Sergeant and will be flown to PNG to continue your service there.' He explained that with independence looming for PNG, the Australian Government was anxious to improve the education standard of the local soldiers of the Pacific Islands Regiment (PIR) so they would be ready to step up to the role of Officers. I had two weeks to prepare, drive my Mini back to Brisbane, say goodbye to my family and fly back to Melbourne for departure for Port Moresby.

On a cold August night at 10 pm a group of young army teachers set off for PNG. It was freezing when we left Melbourne and we were dressed in full winter Battle Dress. After completing the 'milk run' stopovers in Sydney and Brisbane, we arrived in Port Moresby at 6 am the following day. As I looked out of the window of the aircraft I saw the local natives walking around with just a rami (lap lap), or shorts and no shirts. Geez, I thought, they are certainly tough, until they opened the doors of the plane. The heat hit us like a blast furnace and the humidity was about 80%. We couldn't wait to get to the barracks and strip off.

With some of the others I was taken to Murray Barracks. As everything had happened so quickly the barracks were not exactly prepared for us, especially where accommodation was concerned. The only accommodation was in Besser Block huts which had recently been constructed as married quarters for the local soldiers. They were referred to as LEP's, and were two bedroom units with a shower and toilet, but no cooking facilities. This was expected to take place outside in true Papuan style. To accommodate four men they had sectioned off part of the main living area using steel cupboards. Somehow I must have drawn the long straw because I managed to get one of the two bedrooms. Furniture was basic. A steel bed plus green mosquito net, a steel cupboard and a bedside locker similar to those found in hospitals at the time

Sgt. P. Wedgwood, Papua New Guinea, 1966.
Photo courtesy P. Wedgwood.

Each LEP was provided with a wash/iron boy, a local man whose job it was to do all our laundry, cleaning and generally look after us. We didn't even have to polish our own boots! All meals would be taken in the Sergeant's Mess. We were provided with the local uniform known as Juniper greens, consisting of shirt, shorts, knee length socks and a beret.

Early PIR classroom. *Photo courtesy P. Wedgwood*

My first challenge in teaching native soldiers came with their lack of English. We were given texts that said things like, 'I am now opening the door'. We were supposed to demonstrate this but as our 'classroom' was an open-sided marquee that was difficult.

As a science teacher it was also my task to try to get these soldiers to the equivalent of the Queensland Junior Certificate (grade 10 nowadays). Most of them had barely completed primary school. I swiftly learnt to be innovative.

There were many regulations which I had been unused to in Australia, mainly around the possibility of contracting malaria. It was compulsory to wear long pants and long sleeved shirts after 6 pm, even when in civvies. Entertainment in Port Moresby was fairly limited. There were functions provided at the Mess, with local dance bands performing on a regular basis and darts competitions. In the town there was a choice of two cinemas or the local drive-in. Going to the pictures, dressed up like a turkey marked one out immediately as belonging to the Army.

The regular WO2 was quite a character, who took pity on 'the boys away from home' and decided that we should experience as much as possible of what Port Moresby and further afield had to offer. He organised a boat trip out on the harbour, trips up to the rubber plantations outside the town, charter flights to Popondetta (near Kokoda) to see coffee and cocoa being grown and processed, and a trip to Tapini.

On a personal note I purchased a small reel-to-reel tape recorder and communicated with my family in Brisbane in that way. My Dad was always keen to hear my impressions, comparing them to his time in Port Moresby between 1942 and 1944.

Through the efforts of the local Church of England minister, another Nasho and I joined the choir of St John's Church. In late October, the daughter of the choir director/organist returned from an overseas trip. In only a short time the two of us became 'serious' and we were married the following May. The end of my barracks life!

We still had to do training ourselves and one such time was spent at the Goldie River training depot. We spent three very hot, humid days decked out in jungle greens, including revolting canvas boots, weapons training and navigating through the jungle. As result of the boots I subsequently lost my toenails – they simply fell off. I remember very clearly one of the local soldiers firing the automatic rifle version of the SLR. We were supposed to let off small bursts, but this fellow kept his finger on the trigger with the result that the rifle took over and began to spray everywhere. As it was live ammunition soldiers were running in all directions to escape being hit. Luckily no one was injured.

Another memory is the pride the local soldiers took in their uniform. One soldier lining up for parade had another ironing out the creases in his shirt with a hot iron while he stood there.

To those Nashos who served in Vietnam our time in PNG must seem idyllic. However, I like to think as a group we did contribute in some small way to providing PNG with a competent Defence Force when independence came in 1975.

My group was the first and others followed. They have now formed an Association known as Chalkies, to keep the memories alive. Their experiences were different to ours as proper accommodation was supplied plus superior teaching facilities, all thanks to the Australian Government of the day.

Pam and I left PNG in November 1967, costing the Army considerably more to transport the goods (including a car) of a married Nasho back to Australia, than it had to send me up there in the first place. The Army was still to feature in my life back in the civilian world. In 1969 I applied for, and received, a Special Scholarship from the Army which enabled me to take a year off from Queensland Education and complete another full year of my science degree at UQ with all expenses paid. I finished the degree in 1972 studying part time. In 1989 I became an Officer in the 13 Regional Cadet Unit here in Toowoomba until my retirement in 2005.

16
BIRTH IN TOOWOOMBA OF THE NATIONAL SERVICEMEN'S ASSOCIATION OF AUSTRALIA (NSAA)

ALLEN CALLAGHAN AND NOEL WALLIS

On 28 November 1987 the late Barry Vicary and a group of Nasho friends met in a Toowoomba park to form the NSAA. They were Vietnam era National Servicemen and Barry was seeking a better deal for them including health and housing benefits, and a medal recognising their service.

Barry, a concrete and landscape contractor, died suddenly in 1991 of a heart condition leaving behind his wife Mary and eight children.

There had been a small Ex-National Servicemen's Association in Rockhampton but they had different aims and declined to merge with the NSAA. They did, however, allow the new organisation to use their badge.

Nasho group meeting in a Toowoomba Park to form the NSAA, 28 November, 1987. *The Chronicle Archive/APN.*

At first the founding Committee in 1988 were unaware of the extent of the earlier and larger National Service scheme until Dr Noel Wallis applied to join. Barry immediately widened the Association to include the 1950's Nashos.

Don Richards, the first South Australian President, refined the badge by replacing the Federation Star with a Crown, placing the tri-service badge over a map of Australia and re-arranging the wording.

The initial badge was red but each State Branch was allowed to choose its own colour, hence the pale and dark blue badges.

The Initial NSAA badge. *Photo courtesy R. Parsons*

South Australia, the first State Branch outside Queensland, was formed in 1993. This branch was made up almost entirely of first-scheme Nashos. The first Victorian branch was formed at Mildura on 31 October 1993 with Bill Crosbie as President. He became State President with the formation of the Victorian Branch on 27 November 1994. The New South Wales Branch was formed on 24 September 1995 with Michael Skewes as President. The West Australian Branch was formed on 22 November 1996 with Oliver Lovelle as President. The Tasmanian Branch was formed in February 1997 with Ian

McDonough as President and the Northern Territory Branch was formed in July 2005 with Bob Crowell as President.

The NSAA has several unusual features. The Queensland Branch technically is a sub-branch of the founding Toowoomba Branch. The Victorian Branch technically is a sub-branch of Mildura and New South Wales of Broken Hill.

The South Australian Branch was formed independently and learnt a month later of the Queensland Branch. In September 1994, the first interstate meeting of South Australia (including the Broken Hill sub-branch), Queensland and the Mildura sub-branch at the Mildura RSL Club elected Don Richards as President. In 1996 the first meeting of full State Branches elected Barry Presgrave as National President.

The first national event in which the Association participated was the entombment of the Unknown Soldier at the Australian War Memorial in Canberra on11 November 1993. The invitation meant that National Servicemen and the NSAA had been officially recognized. South Australia, Queensland and Broken Hill participated. Similarly, in 2001, National Servicemen were invited to form a contingent in the Army's Centenary Parade in Canberra.

Although the NSAA was founded in Queensland, it was South Australia that moved for incorporation and that is why the National Association is registered in that State. Due to the independent formation of State branches there was no uniform Constitution and each State retains its own. Queensland is the only State that restricts voting rights to National Servicemen.

From Toowoomba, the NSAA spread Australia-wide and is recognised by the Federal and State Governments, Government Departments, the media and other ex-service organisations as the voice of a major segment of the ex-service community. This has resulted in the award in 2001 of the Anniversary of National Service 1951-1972 Medal in recognition of the contribution National Servicemen made to Australia's defence effort for three decades. The Australian Defence Medal was awarded in 2006. The Federal Government also contributed $150,000 towards the National Service Memorial at the right hand entrance to the Australian War Memorial in Canberra.

This is an edited version from 'The National Servicemen's Association of Australia, A History 1987 – 2007' by Allen Callaghan and Noel Wallis. Copyright NSAA (Q) Inc. 2007

Barry Vicary, Founder of the NSAA. *The Chronicle Archive/APN.*

17
THE NSAA FOUNDING SECRETARY REMEMBERS

LAWRIE ASGILL
NSAA FOUNDING SECRETARY 1988-1991
NSAA SECRETARY/TREASURER 1991-1994
NSAA QUEENSLAND LIFE MEMBER AND
PATRON OF THE TOOWOOMBA SUB BRANCH

Back in January 1988 I heard Barry Vicary being interviewed on a local radio station wanting to get as many Nashos together for Anzac Day. I phoned him and we discussed his plan on forming an Association for National Servicemen. I then joined him and around 25 other Nashos to march for the very first time on Anzac Day under our own Banner, the Ex National Servicemen's Association 1965-1972. Not long after Barry asked me to be the Association's first Federal Secretary. Dennis Connon was our Treasurer, Keith Jannusch was Vice President with Barry being President. At this point in time we had around 50 members across Australia, and our Brisbane members were looking at becoming our first sub branch. Little did we know at the time what lay ahead of us. Barry's untimely death in 1991 threw a massive spanner in the works for the Association, would we survive?

NSAA members march on Anzac Day for the first time under their own banner, Toowoomba, 1988. *Photo courtesy L. Asgill*

It is fairly well-known how the Association came about, it's been well documented over the years. But how did the Toowoomba Sub Branch come about, after being the Federal Headquarters of the Association? This is a story I have rarely told.

Back in 1994 when we in Toowoomba gave up our National responsibilities, and when the Brisbane Sub Branch were undertaking a total restructure to become the State Office and South Australia being the new Federal Office, we here in Toowoomba were in a state of limbo. We effectively had no members wanting to be involved in what appeared at the time to be a sinking ship. Dennis Connon had just moved away and I was left holding the bag. Through a sense of loyalty to our founder Barry Vicary, I continued running business as normal. At this time Brisbane and I were continually liaising with each other on a number of issues. The main issue was for Toowoomba to become the first sub branch of the new State Office of Queensland.

For this to happen we needed an active group of members which we didn't have. ANZAC Day was still well supported, and from this support I had a list of Nashos' names. From these there were about 8 Nashos who allowed me to use their names in any correspondence to Brisbane. These Nashos were sympathetic to my cause, but none could physically help me. We had a 'Claytons' sub branch for over 12 months. I avoided meetings between the two groups by making all types of excuses. As I said before I only had names to use, no actual bodies. Then one day I couldn't get away with it any longer, the now new Brisbane State Office was going ahead at full steam and they were coming to Toowoomba to present the Toowoomba group with their charter to make us the first sub branch of the newly formed Queensland National Servicemen's Association. Also the new State President was going to present Mary Vicary with one of the new Nasho medals minted by South Australia. I booked the RSL Hall and made all the arrangements. It was going to be a big day.

A few weeks earlier a work mate of mine, John Larkin, was the first to offer me some help. Unknown to me prior to this, John was a 1950's Nasho and he volunteered to take on the role of Secretary, a position he held for 12 months.

As there was no one else, I was going to take on the dual roles of President/Treasurer which under Incorporation is not allowed. Anyway, in an effort to get as much support as possible

I phoned as many Nashos from my list that I could. There were about 15 to 20 Nashos coming from Brisbane so I needed a good turnout. To say I was a bit worried would be an understatement. Thankfully, quite a few Toowoomba Nashos turned up on the big day. Even some of the ones whose names I used were also in attendance.

Just prior to the State President arriving, John Ford approached me. At the time I didn't know John, and he asked me a few questions about the Association. When John realised we didn't have a Treasurer he said, 'do you want one?' To which I quickly replied YES, and John was immediately appointed Treasurer. Within about a minute our new State President arrived and walked straight over to us, and I was able to proudly introduce our Treasurer.

I had just pulled off the biggest scam of my life and had come through the other side laughing. Toowoomba was about to get going, again! To this day the State Office still doesn't know that their first sub branch was effectively formed on that very day. From this day we were able to gain a reasonable amount of press coverage and we had a fairly good roll-out of potential new members. The hard work was about to begin. At our very first meeting plans were put into place to attract more members. Those in attendance were also asked to assist us financially by making a $5 donation. We now had money in the bank. If memory serves me right, Bryce Rodgers suggested we have a barbecue at the Lions Park at Hodgsonvale which was very well-attended, and we got some more new members. From these first few gatherings the Sub Branch was able to attract a number of future outstanding members who were keen to get involved.

Not long after this, Brisbane told us they wanted Toowoomba to host the inaugural State Conference. Could we do it? I asked the meeting and all were keen to get into it boots and all. So we established a committee to oversee proceedings. Where do you start in organising an event as large as a State Conference? We had no guidelines to follow. None of the group had done anything potentially this large. Thankfully quite a few of our new members had a wealth of experience and knowledge, so we had a good starting point. It was a steep learning curve for us all.

First up we had a Friday night meet and greet at the RSL. Registration and the Conference were held at the University of Southern Queensland in Toowoomba, and the Saturday night dinner dance (with the Countdowns) was also held at the USQ. Brigadier Boxhall was our guest speaker, and he gave a speech that made you want to run out to enlist again. Stirring stuff indeed. It was one of the best night's out I'd had for quite a while. Big Ross Fisher arranged for buses to transport members to the dinner and take them back to their motels. Everything went off so well.

We also thought it would be a good idea to hold a reunion and barbecue on the Sunday after the Memorial Service at the Mothers Memorial. Our then new Secretary, Brian McNamara, was able to source a large supply of meat and bread rolls, etc, for the barbecue at no cost. More money in the bank! At the end of proceedings Leo Camm auctioned off the surplus meat, most of which sold for more than the recommended retail price. More money in the bank!

I believe Toowoomba made the template and set the benchmark for all future State Conferences. I still have people to this day remind me that the first State Conference was the best ever. I won't enter into that debate. Maybe it was regarded as the best ever because it was the very first State Conference and everything was new.

There were no guidelines given to me on how to run a sub branch. I drew on my experiences with the Toowoomba Motorcycle Club, of which I'm also a Life Member. It's my belief that everyone is entitled to a fair go and to be treated with respect and fair play. I made it very clear that if you had a hidden agenda, were aggressive or had an ego, you left it at the door, or you were not welcome.

I also believe that for us to be regarded as a genuine ex-service group we had to get involved with other ex-service groups in Toowoomba. One of the first things I decided was to allow any member (not just the executive) the right to lay wreaths at memorial services, and to become both socially and actively involved with other ex service groups. Through our activity within the local ex-service groups we established a reputation as a 'can do' sub branch and were regarded by our peers as fair dinkum blokes, not 'want-to-bes', as some Nashos have been referred to.

The 'can do' attitude displayed by the Toowoomba Nashos over many years has made our Sub Branch one of, if not the most highly regarded Sub Branch in the State and Nationally. We have had members on the State Executive Committee and on the National Committee.

After I was appointed Chairman of the State Memorial Committee to construct our State Memorial, quite a few of the Toowoomba Sub Branch members were the first to volunteer to be on the Committee and assist me in the funding, planning and construction of our State Memorial located in the Mothers Memorial precinct.

Over the years Toowoomba Branch has achieved a great deal, and we can all be very proud of our achievements. The support shown to me by both the Toowoomba Sub Branch and those on the State Committee over the years has meant a great deal to me, and continues to fill me with pride to this day.

Finally, as stated previously, the membership of the Toowoomba Nashos has made our Sub Branch one of the most highly regarded sub branches in Queensland and Nationally.

SERVICEMEN'S
NATIONAL
ASSOCIATION
51
72
NAVY · ARMY · AIRFORCE

18
THE TOOWOOMBA AND DISTRICT BRANCH

THE BRANCH NEWSLETTER

The first edition of the Toowoomba Branch newsletter, NASHO NOTES, was sent to members in May, 1998. It covered rifle shooting results, a bus trip to Clifton, future events, meetings and recruitment, etc. It was written by Dennis Gillbard who was the Editor until 2005 when Alan Beckerley took over for a brief time.

The current Editor, Gordon Meiklejohn, took over in 2006 and expanded the Newsletter to eight pages. Published bi-monthly, it is the primary means of communicating with members who hail from all parts of the region.

MEMBERS' WELFARE

The duties of a welfare officer in any organisation can range from regular informal contact with a few recipients, with support and assistance from local executive and branch members, to highly responsible and complex matters dealt with by a welfare team in a large organisation. The job of a Nasho Branch Welfare Officer is a relatively simple matter of identifying needs and providing a 'first response' to that need as well as providing support and reassurance to the member or family concerned. The Welfare Officer should have a network of contacts to ensure he is one of the first to respond. The need may vary from assistance with household and gardening chores, monetary help in a crisis, hospital visits, Nasho Funeral rituals, or arranging medical aid and counselling where necessary. Recently the Branch provided a motorised wheelchair to a disabled member. At Branch level everyone knows just about everyone else and the camaraderie which exists ensures that whatever can be done is done, in the shortest possible time without any fuss.

The concept is simple, but requires a high level of empathy, sound commonsense and a willingness to spend time, which might otherwise be leisure time, attending to the needs and wants of Nasho members temporarily unable to cope with a situation. Welfare also encompasses day-to-day companionship and activities which ensure members are not isolated and have fulfilling lives as far as practicable. An active social committee is of vital importance in this matter.

These are the thoughts of one not highly-qualified Welfare Officer, who would like to add the final unnecessary remark that we are each 'Our Brother's Keeper' and the wellbeing of mates is the business of every member.

PRESENTATION OF MEDALS

On 19 May 2002 over 100 local Nashos from both the Korea and Vietnam eras were presented with their Anniversary of National Service 1951-1972 Medals by the Minister for Industry, Tourism and Resources and Federal Member for Groom, Mr Ian Macfarlane. Held at the Toowoomba RSL Hall, the function was organised by our Branch with considerable help and co-operation from Mr Macfarlane's Office.

A second presentation was organised later in November for those who missed out the first time.

When the Australian Defence Medal was awarded in 2006, Nashos were eligible for that medal and so a further Presentation Ceremony was held.

It has taken a long time but the award of these two medals to Nashos for their service to their Country is tangible official recognition.

FUNDRAISING STALLS

Since its early days the Toowoomba Branch has organized barbecues, art unions and raffles, etc., to raise funds. In 1995 Les Robinson, after watching sales of badges and poppies at an RSL Remembrance Day stall in a shopping centre, suggested our members also set up stalls. Les and the Branch Secretary, Kevin Sullivan, organised stock, tables and signage once members agreed, then venues were booked. Over the

Presentation of medals by Ian Macfarlane MP, Federal Member for Groom, 2002. *Photo courtesy L. Robinson*

Australian Defence Medal and Anniversary of National Service 1951 – 1972 Medal. *Photo courtesy R. Parsons*

NSAA Toowoomba and District stall, Clifford Gardens Shopping Centre, 2013. *Photo courtesy L. Robinson*

Qld. National Service State Memorial Sub-Committee, 2003. *Photo courtesy L. Robinson*

The Mega Garage Sale, October, 2003. *Photo courtesy L. Robinson*

The Queensland National Service State Memorial, Toowoomba.
Photo courtesy Joyce McNeil.

NSAA Toowoomba and District Branch Laurel Wreath.
Photo courtesy R. Parsons

The Branch Honour Board. *Photo courtesy R. Parsons*

years the stalls have been a great success. The sites have had to change from time to time and it hasn't always been easy to get volunteers for various reasons. Dennis Gillbard currently manages this activity and has stalls operating at Grand Central, Clifford Gardens and The Range Shopping Centres on the days leading up to Anzac Day and Remembrance Day each year.

THE SERVICE RIFLE SHOOT

Rifle shooting in the NSAA Toowoomba Branch began in the late 1990's when a few Nashos joined with members of The Sporting Shooters Association at a small range at Geham near Cabarlah. Membership grew to 9 and became The Service Rifle Shoot using .303 rifles identical to those issued to National Servicemen in the 1950's.

A shoot was held on the third Sunday each month and the winner was presented with the Monthly Medal.

When the Geham Range was closed down our group relocated to the Sporting Shooters Complex at Captain's Mountain near Millmerran. The complex is extensive with a variety of ranges and modern facilities.

In 2002 Les Robinson made a shield named 'The Cock of the Walk' which is presented every year to the shooter who wins the Monthly Medal the most times in that year. When participants in our monthly shoot fell to 3, invitations were extended to Vietnam era Nashos.

THE QUEENSLAND NATIONAL SERVICE STATE MEMORIAL

What started out in January 2002 as a modest plan to erect a plaque on a rock for Toowoomba Nashos culminated in the unveiling of the State National Service Memorial in Toowoomba on Sunday, 24 October, 2004.

At the same time that the Toowoomba Branch of the National Servicemen's Association began looking at the possibility of a small Memorial, there was also a larger plan under way by the State body to erect the Queensland State Memorial.

At a subsequent State Conference, it was suggested that the State Memorial should be built in Toowoomba, rather than Brisbane, because the National Servicemen's Association was founded here. This suggestion received support from among the 33 Branches statewide and as a result of a members' vote at a later State Conference in Townsville in March, 2003, Toowoomba was chosen as the site for the State Memorial. In April of that year, the State Memorial Sub-Committee was formed in Toowoomba and proceeded to call for designs for the Memorial to be submitted for consideration. The final designs were put to a vote of members statewide and the winning entry was by Mr René Rime, a professional designer of Toowoomba.

The Memorial was to be finished in South Australian Imperial Black granite and stainless steel. Chris Calcutt was discovered exhibiting his impressive stainless steel sculptures at the annual Lions Craft Show in Toowoomba and he agreed to have a look at the plans and to meet with the designer who was also at the Exhibition. The contract for the monumental stonework went to J H Wagner & Sons and Chris Calcutt was contracted to provide the Stainless Steel artwork. Toowoomba City Council was supportive of the project since its inception and provided advice and assistance through the Parks and Recreation Department. J H Wagner and Sons, in conjunction with the designer and the stainless steel artist, produced a magnificent Memorial for the 212 National Servicemen killed on active service. The Navy, Army and Air Force are all represented by the different elements of the design.

Fundraising was kicked off by an investigation into the various grants available for this type of project. This included Department of Veterans' Affairs, RADF, Arts Council Grants, various Queensland Government grants and the Gambling Community Benefit Fund. We applied for a grant from the Department of Veterans' Affairs under their Saluting Their Service Scheme and subsequently received the maximum amount available which was $4,000. Branches and individual members of the Association contributed the largest proportion of the donations.

All 32 branches (at the time) throughout Queensland were invited to participate in a Statewide Mega Garage Sale on 10 - 11 October, 2003. Some branches chose to contribute money rather than to organize a garage sale in their areas. The Brisbane Branches held a combined sale at State Headquarters. Some branches set about fundraising by holding raffles locally and the State Management Committee held a Statewide Raffle which returned $14,150 for the Memorial. Several RSL Branches and Service Organisations also made generous contributions.

We were extremely grateful for the generous donations and price reductions given to us by J H Wagner & Sons, which significantly reduced the overall costs. Wagner Investments also gave us a 50% reduction in the cost of materials for the foundations.

When it looked like we were destined to be unsuccessful in our applications to the Gambling Community Benefit Fund, (GCBF), we sent out appeal letters to every politician in Queensland, State and Federal, seeking contributions or assistance. This proved ultimately to have been very timely, as not only did it produce some much needed funds, but it appeared as though our approach may have moved a few mountains behind the scenes as well. The Minister for Works, Housing and Racing, Mr Robert Schwarten, made a donation of $3,000 'in-kind' available through QBuild in Toowoomba which went towards the cost of lighting and landscaping.

As the dedication of the Memorial was scheduled to coincide with the celebrations of the Centenary of Toowoomba City on 24 October, 2004, it was a relief when the GCBF Grants were announced in September and we found that we had received $15,000 for stonework for the Memorial. We had reached the point of no return if the Memorial was going to be completed on schedule. The total cost of the Memorial and associated works was over $79,500 plus around $10,000 in discounts and 'in-kind' donations.

The National Service State Memorial was unveiled on Sunday, 24 October, 2004 by the Hon. Ian Macfarlane, Minister for Industry, Tourism and Resources, on behalf of the Prime Minister Mr John Howard. At 10.30 am on a fine but hot morning, over 300 former Nashos marched from the Lindsay Street Oval in Queens Park along Margaret Street to the Memorial site, led by the National Servicemen's Pipes and Drums, followed further back in the parade by the Range Highland Pipe Band from Toowoomba.

The Hon. Ian Macfarlane took the salute assisted on the dais by the Mayor of Toowoomba, Councillor Dianne Thorley,

NSAA State President Colin Bell, and Bill Mason, State President of the RSL. Nashos travelled from as far afield as Cairns and Victoria to take part in the celebrations. Around 2,500 people attended the Dedication Ceremony held in East Creek Memorial Park in Toowoomba. As the March and Dedication Ceremony were part of the Official Toowoomba Centenary Celebrations, the company was called to order by the Town Crier, Mr Ralph Cockle.

Leo Camm, former Toowoomba Branch President and State Memorial Committee Member, acted as Master of Ceremonies. Prayers were led by Rev. Matthew Weatherley, Chaplain Terry Egan DCM, and Dr Noel Wallis. The Ode of Remembrance was recited by Mr Bill Mason, State President of the RSL. The Last Post and Rouse were executed by Bugler Mr Edgar Kemp. The Harlaxton RSL Brass Band provided the music for the hymn and anthem as well as a short program of concert music for the entertainment of the assembly before and after the Ceremony. Wreaths were laid in honour of the 212 National Servicemen who died on active service. The wreath layers were led by the Hon. Ian Macfarlane who placed a wreath on behalf of the Prime Minister and Government of Australia.

Among the official guests was Mrs Mary Vicary, the widow of Barry Vicary who founded the National Servicemen's Association in Toowoomba in 1987. Also present were the adult children of the founding treasurer Dennis Connon, and the Chairman of the State Memorial Committee Lawrie Asgill. The designer of the Memorial Mr René Rime, the Stonemason Mr Michael Wagner of J H Wagner & Sons, and the stainless steel sculptor Mr Chris Calcutt were official guests, as were many business people who had made a significant contribution to the cost of the Memorial.

A large number of Toowoomba Councillors and local Members of Parliament were also present. Member for Toowoomba North Mr Kerry Shine also represented Mr Robert Schwarten, State Minister for Public Works, Housing and Racing. Following the official Ceremony, members and guests moved back to the Lindsay Street Oval for lunch.

A video of the March and Dedication was made for posterity.

THE LAUREL WREATH AND THE HONOUR BOARD

At the time Keith Shepherd joined our Branch in 1997 we were low on funds. One expense was for wreaths to lay on Anzac Day, Armistice Day, etc. Keith noticed some Ex-Service organisations had nicely-carved wooden ovals to which a bunch of flowers could be attached at the rear. After a Service the flowers were detached and the wooden oval recovered.

Keith suggested we do the same and volunteered to make something really special. Based on the laurel leaf head-dress of Caesar Augustus in ancient Rome he got to work using cedar that he had recovered from the old Manual Telephone Exchange in Charleville when he was installing an Automatic Exchange there in the early 1980's.

Impressed with his workmanship, Keith was given a letter of appreciation from the Branch and asked to be the custodian of the wreath, for which he later made a carrying case.

At a meeting some time after the wreath was made it was suggested that the Branch should have an Honour Board and again Keith volunteered. Made of heritiera actinophylia and maranti with the mount behind the pediment cedar, again from the Charleville Exchange, he based the design on Doric Architecture such as that of the Parthenon in Greece. A small Life Member Board hangs below the Honour Board. Both the Wreath and the Honour Board are highly prized by the Branch.

SOCIAL ACTIVITIES

Bus Trips

During the past 10 years many bus trips have been enjoyed by Toowoomba and District members. All the nooks and crannies around Toowoomba and beyond have been enjoyed. Terry and Pat McGovern were the ones responsible for such great times. They were ably assisted by Barbara Schmidt. Because of their knowledge of the area we have experienced trips to Darling Downs Zoo, Clifton, Nobby, Leyburn, Pittsworth and Ned's Corner just to name a few. All these places were viewed with a wonderful commentary by Terry who seemed to know the area like the back of his hand. We even had the joy of a trip to Brisbane and lunch on the River Queen.

Race Days

Each year Branch members attend Clifford Park on Cox Plate Day. This is a great occasion to dress up and enjoy a wonderful meal. We are also able to play host to our visiting members and their partners from Beaudesert, Bayside and Gold Coast North. Whether you win or lose you go home feeling like a winner because of the atmosphere.

Breakfasts

Over the years we have often enjoyed breakfast at the Toowoomba South Bowls Club and last year we were able to have our race day guests attend. These are fun times and very social.

Widow's Lunch

As we are all getting up in years we are sadly saying our earthly goodbyes to some of our Nashos. It is a great honour for us to host a Widow's Lunch and present the ladies with a beautiful brooch. It allows our Widows to know that the service their husbands gave to National Service is appreciated.

OBE's Lunch

This is a lunch we started to celebrate in 2013. As many of our Nashos are turning 80 it was agreed we should celebrate this milestone. We had 12 OBE (Over Blooming Eighty) Nashos as special guests to the lunch at the Irish Club Hotel. It is hoped over the next few years to have many more celebrations as our Nashos become octogenarians.

Monthly Lunch

Last year one of our members asked if it was possible for us to have a social lunch once a month. Everyone thought this was a great idea and wondered why we had not thought of it before. So we now meet on the third Friday of the month at the City Golf Club. This has become a very successful lunch with an average of 20 members attending. It is just a time for a casual lunch and lots of catching up and fellowship.

Christmas Lunch

No year would be complete without the Christmas Celebration. This usually takes place early in December. It has been held in several places over the years, namely Toowoomba South Bowls Club, City Golf Club, The Royal Hotel and last year we ventured out to Meringandan to the Meringandan Hotel. All these occasions have been fun times. Many thanks go to the ladies that have organized this function and made it such a happy time.

Theatre Nights

The past few years we have dressed up and gone to the Toowoomba Repertory Theatre. This is always a great night enjoyed by all. The Theatre only holds 100 so it is very intimate. The plays they put on are very good and we all look forward to not only an entertaining night but also the wonderful supper put on at intermission.

It should be clear from the foregoing that being part of the Nashos is not all business. We have a very good social life as well. New members and their partners are always welcome.

PLANNING FOR THE FUTURE

In October 2013 the Toowoomba and District Branch hosted a lunch for those members who had turned 80 and presented each one with an OBE (Over Bloomin' Eighty) Certificate. With a few exceptions the first National Service scheme Nashos were born between 1933 and 1941, and the second scheme Nashos between 1945 and 1952. In other words, the Korea period members are Depression or Wartime babies whilst the Vietnam era ones are Baby-Boomers.

The fact that National Service ended in 1972 means that our youngest Nashos are now into their 60's and at some time in the future the NSAA will have to be wound up, unless of course there is a third scheme. One of the outcomes of this is the recent introduction of the monthly social lunches as a way for Nashos to keep in touch after the NSAA ends.

This inevitable situation will sooner or later confront all NSAA branches and much thought is being given to planning for tomorrow.

THE TOOWOOMBA AND DISTRICT BRANCH

The material for this Chapter was submitted by numerous members of the Branch. Their names are included in the Acknowledgements list.

2013 - 2014 OFFICE BEARERS

Patron Lawrie Asgill	President Leo Camm	Vice President Bill Lane	Immediate Past President Terry McGovern

Chaplain Matthew Weatherley	Secretary Pat O'Sullivan	Assistant Secretary Joan O'Sullivan	Treasurer Dennis Gillbard

Newsletter Editor Gordon Meiklejohn	Rifle Shooting Les Robinson	Welfare Officer Frank Giles	Social Organiser Carol Baldwin

Toowoomba and District Branch Office Bearers 2013-2014.
Photos courtesy Gordon Meiklejohn

19
CHAPLAIN'S CORNER

PADRE MATTHEW WEATHERLEY

MY NATIONAL SERVICE EXPERIENCE

At the time I was called-up during the First National Service Scheme, I was working in the Shipping Branch of the Myer Emporium Melbourne and studying the 'Radio Trade Course' at the Royal Melbourne Technical College Night School.

Several years before I learned the Australian Government was going to compulsorily call me up, I joined the Air Training Corps based at North Melbourne, probably because, as a boy, I loved he wartime 'Biggles' stories. At eighteen years of age, having passed my physical, and despite having told the Recruiting Officer I was in the ATC and wanted to join the Air Force, I was called-up for the Army and ordered to report to the Army at Puckapunyal.

It so happened that my ATC Commanding Officer always printed at the bottom of our discharge papers, something like 'If you are called-up for a service you do not wish to be in, come and see me'. So, 'in for a penny, in for a pound', I went and saw my CO, who immediately called me up for the Air Force, ordering me to go to the 6th Unit NST RAAF Point Cook instead, which I did in January 1955.

Air Force Nasho Matthew Weatherley, 1955.
Photo courtesy M. Weatherley

Three months later, 'Dinger' Bell, my CO at Point Cook, called me into his office, asking me, how come I was here? I told him politely and heard no more. Some months later after I had completed initial training, a church mate of mine who trained at Puckapunyal said to me, 'Do you realise you were listed AWOL for about three months and the Military Police were looking for you?'

I thoroughly enjoyed my time at Point Cook. Although we were supposed to be working in the Radio Branch at Point Cook no one seemed to know what to do with us Nashos. It was rumoured at the time that only the Army wanted men, not the Navy and the Air Force.

Even as late as 1955/56, the Federal Government still expected the Korean War to flare up, so much so, that each year the Cadet Officers and NCO's who had nearly completed their flying training were dropped off in a less populated area south-east of Melbourne, Central Gippsland, and had to get back to a certain place without being caught by the Victorian Police and the RAAF MP's. Thus it gave them escape experience.

Each year, some of us Nashos were chosen to assist the Police and MP's to catch the Cadets, by setting up an under-canvas base in Gippsland. In the year I was chosen we never saw a Cadet on the run. However, we were assured by the Police they caught most of them. Two who did get back to their home base were Asian-born. Maybe they'd had more experience back in Asia than the Australian-born ones.

Air Force National Service Trainees, Point Cook Vic. 1955.
Photo courtesy M. Weatherley

While I was there, the Cadet Officers and NCO's were still training in Tiger Moths. However, some of those who had completed the first part of their training had upgraded to Wirraways. On one occasion when I was sweeping the Control Tower floor, a Flight Sergeant came in with an extra parachute, head-gear and goggles in his hands, wanting someone to go with him to just sit in the second seat and enjoy the ride in a Wirraway. He had to get his hours up, probably towards going onto jets. I think Australians had been flying Vampires in Korea.

I was chosen to go up with the Flight Sergeant and enjoyed by first ride in a warplane. After flying at 300 feet between the two peaks of the You Yang Mountains, he did the usual loops and rolls, and then flew up very high and seemed to come screaming straight down so low that a cow looking up and me looking down were both scared stiff. I pleased myself by not throwing up.

I hated having a surname that commenced with "W" because I seldom got chosen for interesting jobs. However, there was one occasion when I was very glad of it. Towards the end of my time at Point Cook, a couple of Nashos got into trouble for doing something wrong, which meant that they had to do the Guard Duty I had been rostered on to do. This meant I never did Guard Duty all my time as a Nasho, so eventually I thanked God for having Weatherley as a surname.

Occasionally we got a week off. On one weekend my false teeth got washed out of my mouth by a big wave at Dromana, so when I got back to base, I was given a pass to go back to Myers Dental Department to get a new set made and fitted.

Sometimes while I was at Point Cook, I rode my Norton Dominator 500cc motor cycle to and from the base. At night on two separate occasions at a particular 'S' bend, I found myself being forced off the Princes Highway on the wrong side of the road onto oncoming traffic. Had I not done so I would not be here today.

I thoroughly enjoyed the whole of my National Service because it gave me a freedom and fellowship with others I never had at home being an only child. The worst thing was firing the .303 rifle because no matter how I tried, being thin I always came away with a very sore, bruised shoulder.

MY DISCOVERY OF AND INVOLVEMENT IN THE NATIONAL SEVICEMEN'S ASSOCIATION

I had no knowledge of the NSAA until I read in the Toowoomba Chronicle of Ian Macfarlane's First Medal Presentation, which ended by inviting 1950's Nashos to contact the Toowoomba Branch Secretary, Kevin Sullivan (now deceased). Early in April 2002 Kevin greatly assisted me in becoming a full member. Probably only the Equipment Officer, Merv Watson, knew I was a priest and had been the Toowoomba Anglican Hospital Chaplain for many years before retirement from full-time ministry. I kept it quiet by not wearing my 'dog collar', because I wanted to be accepted as a fellow Nasho and not singled out and separated from the members.

I found the first meeting I attended on 14 May 2002 in a room of the Toowoomba RSL building to be very interesting. The main discussion centred around the possibility of Toowoomba becoming the home of the State National Service Memorial in the park grounds near the Mother's Memorial, led by Bob and Joyce McNeil, who did a lot of negotiating with the then Toowoomba City Council, very ably supported by the then Mayor Di Thorley.

I received my Nasho Anniversary Medal from Ian Macfarlane at the Second Medal Presentation in the Salvation Army Hall. If it still was not known I was a priest, it came out at the 'Turning of the Sod' to commence construction of our Memorial. As the then Toowoomba Nasho Chaplain, Terry Egan, was seriously ill in hospital, and knowing I was a member, he asked me to Bless and Dedicate the Ground where our Memorial was to be placed.

I had the honour of doing that on Friday 16 July 2004 *(see News Clipping)*. Three months later on 24 October 2004, together with the State Chaplain Dr Noel Wallis, Terry Egan and I had the privilege of 'Blessing and Dedicating the Memorial' free of debt.

'Nashos' stand proud as cit
launches a lasting memoria

By Merryl Miller
merrylm@thechronicle.com.au

BETWEEN the years 1951 and 1972, 287,000 young Australian men were conscripted into this nation's defence forces.

Many "Nashos" died in the service of their country, yet for decades these men remained the forgotten war heroes, scorned at times by those they were sworn to defend.

That was all water under the bridge yesterday, however, when the first sod for the Queensland memorial to National Servicemen was turned in Toowoomba's East Creek Park.

"It's a proud day today — for the community response in getting this happening, and for everyone's efforts in making it a reality," National Servicemen's
Association founding m
Lawrie Asgill, of Toowo
said.

"This helps Nashos fe
part of the overall defenc
munity and acknowledg
integral role we have pla

Toowoomba was chose
site for the memorial b
the association — now t
ond largest ex-servic
organisation after the
was formed by a Toow
man, the late Barry Vica

Estimated to cost $60,
memorial will be unve
October this year.

"It is overwhelming t
these people here today,
fying," Mr Asgill said.

"One hundred and eig
en Nashos were killed
those years, and they ca
all walks of life."

■ **Taking part in the National Service memorial sod-turning ceremony yesterday are (from left) Father Matthew Weatherley, Colin Bell, and Mayor Cr Dianne Thorley.**
Picture: NEVILLE MADSEN

Newspaper clipping of Padre M. Weatherley blessing State Memorial site 2004. *The Chronicle Archive/APN.*

Becoming increasingly unwell, Terry Egan conferred with me and then wrote formally to the Toowoomba Branch asking them to consider accepting me as their Chaplain, which they did. Knowing I had experience in military protocol, soon after this, Terry asked me to design and produce the Annual Commemoration Order of Service. At that time there was an annual march through the streets of Brisbane commemorating the commencement of National Service in 1951, so it became the tradition in Toowoomba to hold our Commemoration service a day or two either side of that on the nearest second weekend in February. Our First Commemoration took place on Saturday 13 February 2005, with Terry giving the address. It was soon after this he passed on.

Three months later in May 2005 I joined the new Highfields RSL Sub-Branch and soon found myself being asked to be their Chaplain, on the understanding that should I be needed at Toowoomba Memorials they would take precedence.

Shortly after I was recognised as the Toowoomba Honorary Chaplain, the then State Chaplain, Dr Noel Wallis, sent me an official copy of the Manual of the Protocol for Funerals of Army National Servicemen. I soon discovered that there are a number of differences when a Nasho was in the Navy or Air Force. In June 2011, I put all this together in one eight page booklet, which includes a form that can be filled out by a person who is leading a Funeral Service, so that the main points of a person's service record are not overlooked. Copies are available from the Toowoomba Branch Secretary. It is produced in such a way that non-clergy can use it.

Because of my varying health and it being a thirty kilometre round trip to Toowoomba for me living at Highfields, I regret my role as Chaplain largely has to be ceremonial. Currently I have the honour and privilege of being the Honorary Toowoomba RAAF-A Branch and the Queensland State

Division RAAF-A Chaplain, all evolving from being asked to be the Toowoomba NSAA Chaplain over a decade ago.

Cheers from Padre Matthew Weatherley.

SERVICEMEN'S
NATIONAL
ASSOCIATION
51
72
NAVY · ARMY · AIRFORCE

20
ANECDOTES

A CONVERSATION WITH A BRIGADIER

Jim Skinner

Out on a march we had stopped for a 10 minute break after marching for fifty minutes. We were laying on our packs in the shade when red-lapelled brass with a considerable escort approached. Everyone jumped up and saluted, that is everyone except me.

I was approached by the number one brass and asked if I was going to salute. My answer was that I was on my 10 minute break but I would salute when that time had elapsed. The brass, I believe, was Brigadier Martin.

He and I then entered into a seven minute conversation. He asked if I liked being a Nasho. Yes, I considered it as a holiday. We discussed the Second World War and why I thought this training was a good idea. I told him that I had ten relatives who returned from World War 2 and that I was the recipient of some alluring stories.

I remember asking Brigadier Martin why I was in the infantry when I had applied for the engineers, as I had been working with machinery such as bulldozers, etc. for some years. The Brigadier said the army has proved that bushmen make the best infantry soldiers.

I accepted his word and could see he was going to make the conversation last until the 10 minutes were up, so at exactly that time I stood up and saluted him. He returned the salute, shook my hand and thanked me for the conversation.

'A' Company 11Bn parade, Wacol, 1951. (Pte. Jim Skinner Row 1 nearest to jeep.) *Photo courtesy J. Skinner*

THE DEMON DRINK

Frank Giles

It was just prior to the start of Spring. The year was 1955. In a small western Queensland town a group of anxious youths attended the Railway Station to meet a commitment to the Federal Government to don the Queen's Uniform. To say that they were not a little apprehensive and excited at the forthcoming prospect might be an understatement. They were National Service Trainees. A regular army soldier was present to call the Roll and make sure all were safely delivered to 11 N.S. Training Battalion at Wacol.

What you may ask was the importance of this occasion that requires recording in history? Simple, I was one of those budding soldiers. I could probably have avoided training due to limited movement of my left arm which had a broken elbow that had not healed properly. The examining doctor asked me if I thought this would impede me from carrying out all soldiering duties. Being young and not very smart I informed this worthy MO it would not be a disadvantage and if necessary I was prepared to salute with my right arm.

A few weeks into training we were allowed local Leave. I now know why some regard freedom with a passion. The occasion was a Dance at Riverview, provided by the local RSL, who made available a host of nubile maidens. My mind was on other things and so were my companions except our mate who owned the car but didn't drink. Did I say 'DRINK'? Not possible, as everyone knows Nashos may not drink and it is a fact that Australian Forces are renowned for their obedience to rules. HA HA. One of our Instructors was sympathetic to our plight and agreed to obtain some bottles of beer. Not to wipe us out, just enough for a 'little drinkie'. With the wisdom of hindsight it was probably not smart to consume these on a suburban street and in proximity to the front of the Dance Hall. But we did.

On the way back to Wacol we consumed the remaining beer. There was a hell of a queue of cars waiting to enter the front gate and some people in red caps seemed to be searching cars. This did not bode well for us so we disposed of the evidence in long grass by the roadside. The MP's turned the car inside out but found nothing. Still they accused us of drinking. We denied everything and protested our innocence. Just who did they think they were? Police or something! Nothing happened so we went to bed.

Next morning we rose as usual, performed the three 'S's and were called to the Company Orderly Room. We were questioned about the previous evening and the allegations. It was further alleged this took place in company with one of our Instructors, Cpl. 'No Name'. What an obvious fabrication. As if us Nashos would fraternise with our tormentor. Later we were invited to Battalion HQ. We didn't get morning tea there either. A very stern Lt. Colonel informed us all that we were in trouble and the best thing for us was to confess, plead guilty and dob in our mate. We had a story and stuck to it.

Unknown to us this Lt. Col. was a Q.C. in private life. He then questioned us individually but we stuck to our guns. Next day it was on again, and again on the third day. On the final occasion he informed me that one of our bunch who was not involved had cracked under cross-examination and did I feel like changing my statement under the circumstances? If the cat is out of the bag it is no good continuing to tell the 'truth' is it! I thought a long time afterwards, after watching Rumpole of The Bailey on TV, that the Legal Fraternity are a cunning bunch. Too smart for a bunch of 'innocent' Nashos.

The final outcome did not involve shooting at dawn but three Battalion Guard duties and about four Company Piquets. It was not so good for our Corporal who was the main target of the exercise anyway. 'Thou shalt not fraternise with the Trainees'. Poor old Corp' suffered a transfer and a temporary demotion, but seemed happy to be back with his regular unit and out of training troublesome boozy Nashos.

AND THE BOYS FROM THE BUSH

Life is full of opportunities. After we had been in Wacol camp for a few weeks and were tough and hardened troops, we were granted weekend Leave. Great for the City boys, go home, see parents and girlfriend. Take off the baggy khakis, put on civvies and go about without those giveaway white epaulet bands. Maybe even go to a pub except the white band down the left side of the face not totally bronzed due to the slouch hat chin strap, is difficult to hide.

What were country lads to do? Go into town, wander around like lost sheep then come back to Barracks to sleep? Yeah, right (NOT). Sudden light comes on! Taxi Rank outside camp! Taxi drivers can go anywhere, why not Roma? Go out the front, find one to take us to Roma. How far? 300 miles. How much? 40 – 50 quid! We found one who would do it for 30 if we fed him and put him up for the night. There were five of us, six quid each. Not too bad, but still 1½ weeks pay, but what the hell. One bloke wanted to go to Miles which meant we could not use the Condamine (Crystal) Highway, famous for broken windscreens.

We follow the Railway line from Dalby, all dirt track but OK it's not our car. By the way it was not a new car but an original model Holden.

Cabbie was younger than most and game, so off we went. Can't remember if it was Friday arvo or Saturday morn'. Must have been Friday because we only had Leave until 2359 Sunday which meant a rush trip. Fate conspired to change that and we had overlooked the Leave Proviso that this was local Leave and only covered Brisbane. We were country boys and 'local' outback could be 100 miles in any direction. We just misunderstood the terminology. So off we went.

Things were OK until the car informed us that it had spent its life on Brisbane trips and was unused to continual highway speeds in excess of 50 mph. The generator went belly up. Got it fixed at Miles. The Cabbie needed a receipt for the Owner to reimburse him. Another light comes on! If the receipt were dated Sunday, we might conceivably be delayed en-route to the extent that we were unable to return to Camp until late Monday. Clever devils! A leaky radiator necessitated another receipt thus reinforcing our tale of misfortune.

We spent a relaxing and satisfactory time at our various homes. My Dad even shouted me a couple of beers. And my Fiancée was suitably overjoyed, but enough said about that. We telephoned and sadly reported our dilemma to the Orderly Room but were rudely asked, 'What were we doing in Roma?' We were ordered to return immediately or sooner. Were we in trouble? You bet! Were we worried? Just a little, but we were certain it was not a Firing Squad offence. Anyway, Aussie soldiers are renowned for going ack willie in two World Wars and we felt we were only keeping up a proud tradition.

On our return, we were invited to the OC's den for a tête-à-tête. Well a listening anyway. Gob shut, heels together, standing stiff and not making eye contact. Yessir, Nosir. Finally we were asked if we had any mitigating pleas to make before sentence was passed. Well being a shy introspective lad I thought it my place to speak for all. I've always suffered from 'foot-in-mouth' disease. I pointed out that we were not to blame and it was the fault of untrustworthy Yellow Cabs. 'No excuse you left the Leave area'. 'Yes but' - (more f.i.m.). Unfair discrimination, City fellas can go home to the bosom of their families (and girlfriends). Even Ipswich and Toowoomba blokes got home. Why shouldn't we? A light bulb moment! The more we/I protested the greater the cost of paying the Piper would be. Shut up Frank.

One Battalion Guard, four Piquets and numerous Dixie Bashings later, all was forgiven. Indeed, it was a 'not to be forgotten event'. Lesson/s well learned:

1 If possible, don't get caught.

2 If caught, don't lie. Keep your mouth shut.

3 Don't try to outsmart them. It only makes them look bad and hate you all the more.

4 Don't grovel, smile and say 'Yes Sir, thank you Sir'. Salute, about turn and march smartly out to face Sar' Major. He is the first and only enforcer of Discipline in the Ranks. You have besmirched his reputation and made him lose face with the Officer Caste. Bad Bad Bad. Now you are in REAL TROUBLE.

Nasho group wearing basic pouches, Ingleburn, Intake 3/54.
Photo courtesy R. Parsons

A SQUARE DEAL

Name withheld by request

The Officer at Ingleburn Camp was inspecting the night guards before they went on duty.

OFFICER: 'You're all well turned out except for your basic pouches. They should be SQUARED like this man's pouches. What have you packed inside your basic pouches private?'

NASHO (Red-faced): 'Er, just stuff sir.'

OFFICER: 'What sort of stuff private?'

NASHO (Who was now panic stricken): 'cndms.'

OFFICER: 'Speak up son so we can all hear!'

NASHO (In a squeaky voice): 'Condoms sir.'

OFFICER: 'CONDOMS? And just what were you planning on doing with all those....those things?'

NASHO (Near to tears): 'Sell them to Nashos going on weekend Leave sir.'

OFFICER (Towering over Nasho): 'You horrible little man. Get rid of them and report to me at 0900 in the morning.'

The other Guard members could no longer control themselves and broke out into fits of laughter.

Private David Laws (centre), Wacol 1952. *Photo courtesy D.Laws*

SOME UNUSUAL MEMORIES OF WACOL IN 1952

David Laws
2 Platoon 'A' Coy
11 Battalion 2nd Intake, Wacol 1952

Being woken up by our Platoon Sergeant bellowing at us, 'Wakey wakey rise and shine, hands off c-cks and on with sox'

Carrying a bed with the occupant still asleep on it out to the parade ground and leaving it there. If the Trainee woke up while we were carrying him out the door we tipped him out and took off.

One Nasho from a wealthy family got lost while we were on a night exercise. Somehow he made it back home to where he lived and slept in his own bed. He arrived back at camp the next morning in a chauffeur-driven limousine.

COMPANY BUGLER

Ronald Parsons

On being called-up for National Service with 13 N.S.T. Battalion in August 1954, I was made 'E' Company bugler. I'd been a bugler in my high school cadet corps and later in the CMF I was a bugler in 17/18 Infantry Battalion.

Occasionally I would cop flak from some Nashos who cursed me for waking them up when I sounded REVEILLE in the morning. My response to that was, 'What are you whinging about? I have to get up before you and go to bed after you, when I've played LIGHTS OUT at night. And I have to do the same training as you. You don't complain when I play COME TO THE COOKHOUSE DOOR.'

At the end of our basic training there was the Passing Out Parade which family and friends could attend. One of the Officers sent for me in my role as bugler and told me I would be required to play RETREAT while the flag was lowered at the parade. There were to be two buglers on the dais with the brass and bigwigs. When I asked how many people would be there he said, 'Two or three thousand.' I gulped and said, 'Maybe it would be better to ask one of the other Company buglers. I don't think I could play in front of that many people.' The Officer looked me in the eye and said, 'If I tell you to eat sh-t you'll eat it. You can ask for pepper and salt to put on it, but you WILL eat it'. I was stuck and there was no way out.

'E' Company Bugler, 13 NST Battalion, Ingleburn, Intake 3/54.
Photo courtesy R. Parsons

Between then and the big day I practised down by the creek at every opportunity. When I was in the cadets the bugle instructor who came to our school had told me to concentrate on hitting the right notes at the start and the finish. It didn't matter so much if you stuffed up in the middle, that would be overlooked or forgiven. As it turned out I got it right on the day.

RE-ENACTMENT OF A DIXIE BASHING PARADE AT A NASHO REUNION

Darryl Hutton
Lance Corporal
11 Battalion Drum Major
2nd Intake Wacol 1954

CORPORAL: 'What a motley, moth-eaten looking crew you are. Did you shave this morning Private?'

NASHO: 'Yes sir.'

CORPORAL: 'Well next time stand closer to the razor. When did you last have a hair cut? Never mind, report to the barber for a COMPLETE job before 0800 hours Monday morning. And when did you last polish those boots?'

NASHO: 'An hour ago sir.'

CORPORAL: 'Like hell you did. You can go on dixie duty for the next three days and I'll expect every one of those dixies, pots and pans to be spotlessly clean and shining like a new two-bob bit.'

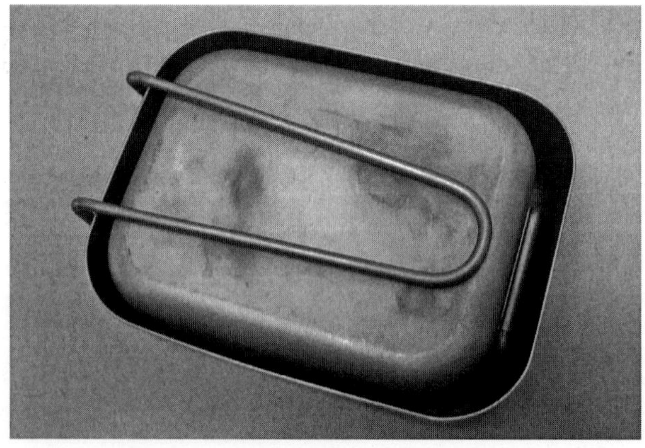

Dixie set. *Photo courtesy R. Parsons*

Nashos Ron Simpson and Darryl Hutton, Wacol, 1954.
Photo courtesy D. Hutton

AUSTRALIAN MILITARY FORCES

AAF A 95
Reprinted Oct, 1953

230

IDENTIFICATION CARD
AND LOCAL LEAVE PASS

No. 1/712761 *Rank* Pte

Name HUTTON D.T.

Unit 102 Coy RAASC (MT)

Whose specimen Signature appears hereon is a member of the above unit and is on local leave as per dates and hours shown on back hereof.

Bearer's Signature D Hutton

Lieut.
ADM & Trg 102 Coy RAASC (MT) *Adjt*
UNIT STAMP

Identification and Local Leave Pass.

Enjoying a meal at Tai-Tung Café Brisbane, while on Local Leave, 1954.
Photo courtesy D. Hutton

AND THE PERILS OF PICKET DUTY

In the fence between the main highway to Brisbane and the Wacol military grounds was a 10 – 12 foot gateway over a dirt road that led to the 'C' Company area, passing by Major Lyons' high-stumped house. From memory, this entrance was not used for wheeled traffic, and as there was not a proper gate, a length of water pipe was used instead. At night a Hurricane Lamp was attached to the middle of the pipe.

On this particular night I was the Nasho NCO-in-charge of the picket of two Nashos (A big responsible job!). Around midnight a taxi cab pulled up at the gateway and out hopped (staggered) our Brass Band instructor, Corporal X. As he approached it was obvious that he had consumed a considerable amount of alcohol. He stopped in front of the piping and said in a drunken tone, 'Raise the bar or I will p-ss (rhymes with bliss) on the lantern!' So the bar with the lamp attached was raised the way it would if a vehicle had to drive through. Corporal X marched through in true military fashion, halted and about-turned as the bar was lowered. He then marched back to the bar and said, 'Well I WILL p-ss on your light anyway'. In doing so he extinguished the lamp's flame.

11 NST Battalion Band, Wacol, Intake 2/54. Drum Major D. Hutton. *Thiel Studio Photo*

A RUDE AWAKENING

Les Robinson

On 10 January 1958 a group of us departed Toowoomba by train bound for National Service in the Army. At Goodna railway station we were picked up by truck and taken to Wacol. On arrival we were ordered to queue up with all our paperwork which was inspected by regular army personnel in a large tent without sides.

The Officer-in-Charge was young like us and just out of Duntroon. One lad had forgotten to bring his paperwork and when called into the tent he said to the Officer, 'Mate I left my paperwork at home.' We all learnt in no uncertain terms not to address an Officer as 'Mate', and that all 'Australian Regular Army Corporals were 'God'. Eventually we were sent to our respective Companies wondering what was in store or us.

Washing, starching and ironing our dress uniforms was an experience and by the time we left Wacol we were pretty good at it. If we attended Church on Sunday morning we were fed burnt chops or steak. If we missed Church we got porridge. The camp's barber had a contract with the Army for which he was paid two shillings and sixpence per haircut. He arranged for trainees to have a haircut every two weeks, which allowed him to afford a 1956 Chev' BelAir.

AND CRIME DOESN'T PAY

In the 1st Intake of 1958 at Wacol after three days of picking up cigarette butts our O.C. – a portly Captain Boyd – took us on a route march through East Wacol. Did we ease up to march up the hills and down the other side? No way, it was RUN UP the hills and RUN DOWN the other side. On arriving back at camp we realised a lot of us were not as fit as we thought we were. Our much older portly Captain was not even breathing heavily enough to blow out a candle and consequently earned a lot of respect. The route march had taken us past a vineyard that was loaded with grapes so a few of us went back that night and filled a couple of haversacks with grapes. However, on returning to our quarters we found that our venture had backfired. The grapes were too green and sour to eat so had to be dumped.

I made a lot of good mates in National Service and still keep in touch with some of them.

COP THIS

Alan Elworthy

After three months' basic training at Ingleburn, south-west of Sydney, I had to report to the 30th Battalion at North Sydney to complete my compulsory military training in the Citizens Military Force (CMF). The 30th Battalion was the NSW Scottish Regiment.

18 Platoon 'E' Company, 13 NST Bn. Intake 3/54 Ingleburn.
(Pte. Alan Elworthy Row 2, 3rd from right.) *Judson Photo*

One weekend we had to go for a shoot at ANZAC Rifle Range. It was pouring with rain and we were supposed to wear work uniform, but not me. I didn't know and turned up wearing the Kilt, but they still made me shoot and cop the bagging. A mate of mine from our Nasho platoon also had to go into the 30th Battalion. When he asked one of the Regulars whether he should wear anything under his Kilt he got the following reply:

'It's like this. On pay night the paymaster sits behind a desk. You march smartly over when your name is called then stand at ease. There is a mirror set in the floor in front of the desk and if the paymaster looks down and sees you are wearing underpants you don't get paid. Does that answer your question?'

After about twelve months I transferred to 2 Div Provos at Victoria Barracks. We were mainly civilian police completing National Service Training. The Regular Army Provos training us did not like Civilian Police and gave us a hard time.

One day during drill our Regular Army Sergeant called us all 'a bag of sh-t'. While we were standing at attention one of the trainees, who was a policeman in civilian life, stepped forward and told the Sergeant he resented being called 'a bag of sh-t' and wanted the Sergeant to redress that wrong. The Sergeant then asked if anybody else resented being called 'a bag of sh-t'. All on parade then stepped forward and said in unison, 'We all resent being called by that name and we all want a redress.'

We were then paraded before our Unit Major and expressed our resentment individually. The result was the Sergeant was ordered to apologise, and boy, was he angry!

Lastly, when we had our Visitors' Day at Ingleburn, my sister and two of her girlfriends came to visit me. The boys from our platoon crowded around and said I had to share and not keep the girls all to myself.

NATIONAL SERVICE IN TASMANIA

Leon Jeffery

I commenced my National Service on 15 August 1955. I had received a *Commonwealth of Australia* letter earlier advising that I had to report to Anglesea Barracks Hobart in 2 weeks' time. After having our letters checked and names ticked off a list we boarded one of the buses for the 20 km trip to Brighton Camp which in those days was out in the wide open spaces north of Hobart. I was familiar with Brighton as I had attended a couple of Army Cadet camps there. We had been instructed to travel lightly taking only toilet gear, writing materials and a Bible, if desired.

After arriving at the camp we were given a Service number and a Platoon number. I was in 3 Platoon. We were allocated to a hut which contained 14 beds, bedside tables and small wardrobes. Recruits from all areas of Tasmania continued arriving over the next day. We were issued with sheets, pillows and blankets as well as eating utensils. The menu was simple, TAKE IT OR LEAVE IT.

We were issued with clothing, boots, shoes, slouch hat, beret and webbing packs. For our training we wore World War 2 style uniforms which were flannel and were handed down from one Intake to the next. They fitted where they touched! Our Platoon Commander was 2nd Lt. Peter Barrie and our Platoon Sgt. was a Korean Veteran, Sgt. Thompson. Cpl's Bell and Innes were both WWII men. L/CPL 'Bully' Hayes arrived shortly after, he came straight from Korea.

Brighton in winter is a very cold place with snow on the surrounding mountains and a chilly wind blowing across the plains. Our washing would freeze on the line overnight. Our training followed the routine procedure for all battalions and at the end of 98 days we were a physically fit, well-trained unit having had many treks of 40 km across the countryside and over mountain ranges carrying our packs.

AS WE SEE IT

We're camped at a place called Brighton
Where it's always sunny and hot
Where the winds don't blow, we never see snow
And the beds are just like cots

We've been here just on three months
We've marched a hundred miles
The boys they all are weary
But their faces still bear a smile

We're all so very footsore
But we don't give a damn
We'll outdo those puny Corporals
And tame them like a lamb

We've almost got the Bomber
And Glover's shout is hoarse
We'll have them calling quits
Before we leave the force

The Officers too are weakening
Under the terrible strain,
Of trying to teach us Slope Arms
But at that we've won again

And at this Camp at Brighton
We've Smith a Second Lieut.,
He's short and neat with great big feet
And a dread to each recruit

Lord Nelson's our Sar' Major
He always falls us in,
Upon the Company parade ground
Without him it's a sin

Lieutenant Bonnett is always there
To lend a helping hand,
And for his tireless work with us
We're the finest in the land

Bill Nimmo and Terry Pears
18 NST Battalion, 3 Platoon, A Company, No. 6 Intake
Brighton, Tasmania, 1953

THE WRECKERS

Roy Payne

The inhabitants of Hut 4 at Brighton became known as 'the wreckers' after the ceiling collapsed from the weight of empty beer bottles stored in it awaiting to be smuggled out of camp and disposed of. The boys worked out how to go under the fence and sneak down the road to the pub for a few long necks, but couldn't work out a way to get rid of the empties.

THIS GOES WITH THAT

Ross Horne

In all walks of life I think we remember the more colourful characters and there are some people we remember more than others. At Singleton, NSW, Army Camp in 1966 we had a training instructor that probably enjoyed a drink more than most people and at times had memory losses.

I distinctly remember most of us doing the M60 machine gun lesson with him and he could never remember the names of the parts of the gun. So it went something like this, 'This part here fits into this part here and are fixed together like that and Bob's your uncle.'

I think not one of us has forgotten that particular lesson mainly because it was unusual. The end result was we still couldn't tell you what parts went into what parts. However, we knew exactly how they worked and by the time he had finished with us we could strip an M60 machine gun with the light on or off, day or night.

NEEDLES DAY AND THE AFTERMATH

Don Weimer

We had been in the Army for three weeks without being allowed visitors or Leave. It had been a lot of hard work on the parade ground trying to make us even half-way resemble soldiers, or not to make a total disgrace of ourselves.

Tomorrow was Visitors Day, but before that we had to receive our first lot of anti-everything needles. This was Intake 1/54, 20 Platoon, Easy Company Wacol. For those who know Wacol, E Company was situated on the far eastern side of the Battalion area. Our 6 needles (3 in each arm) were to be administered in the RAP, which was situated near A Company and B Company on the far western side. Of course you will believe me when I tell you that the Army supplied buses for the trip. Like fun they did! We were required to march, at least 2 miles, in parade-ground fashion.

Like always – it was hurry up and wait, at least one hour standing in the sun. When it finally became our turn, we were shuffled (oops! I mean marched) in single file into the RAP. We were told to remove our shirts and move forward with our arms akimbo.

There were no niceties in those days of a separate needle for each person. They used the same metal and glass needle until it was so blunt that it wouldn't even pierce a baby's butt.

Now here is one of the major points of this story. Several of the blokes collapsed when they received their needles. Not me! It was my mate behind me who suffered most when seeing me get jabbed. We hadn't seen each other for many years but met up again in 1999 at the Wacol Passing-out Parade. Noel then reminded me that he swears the needle bent into a distinct bow before it pierced my skin.

On moving out of the RAP we were instructed to wave, swing or pump our arms to increase circulation of the serum through our system. What a sight it must have been for the next platoon in line.

After we had assembled again we were marched back to our quarters. No huts in those earlier Intakes, we were in long marquees. A total of 48 in the platoon with two marquees, 12 pipe and chain wire bunks on each side. There was a large expanse of gravel, many gum trees and a little grass on the outside. When we arrived back we were told that we had to make our platoon area neat and tidy for our visitors the next day. That meant leaves to be raked, gravel paths to be broomed and every vestige of rubbish to be removed. A super 'Emu Bob'.

The second major point of the story shows some rare compassion on the part of our Platoon NCO's. We were told that if we felt sick, and there were many such genuine cases, we could knock off and go and lie down. And NO penalty would be forthcoming. Many in the platoon immediately went to their bunks. Not I, needles have never worried me. So choosing what I thought would be the easiest task I grabbed a rake and set to on the leaves. My mate Noel also chose the leaves option and there we were side-by-side doing a sterling job. Every now and again we noticed that one of the blokes would go all wobbly and wander off to either the ablutions or his bunk. A short time later I realised what was happening and drew my mate's attention to the fact that the two of us appeared to be the only ones still on our feet.

Guess how many leaves got raked after that!

ANYONE FOR TENNIS?

David Ross

Approximately sixty-five National Service trainees formed the first Intake at No.10 (GR) Squadron, RAAF Base Garbutt, Townsville, from 30 July 1951 to 21 January 1952.

When we had no night Leave, off-duty nights were mostly spent playing night tennis on the courts at the Base. Courts, nets, lighting and balls were rent-free. There was no hit and giggle; many of the players were really good.

One evening a trainee, mustered as a cook hand, finished his Cook House duties and came up for a hit before going to bed. He was very good and we told him so. He said, 'You think I'm good? I've got a little brother back home who is going to be a world beater.' That National Service trainee from the Cook House came from Rockhampton. His name was Trevor Laver and his little brother back home was to become 'Rocket' Rod Laver.

IN THE SIGS

Kyle MacLeod

My being called-up for National Service in the 3rd Intake at 11 Battalion Wacol in 1954, greatly upset my mother. I was her only son with four younger sisters, our father having died as a P.O.W. on the infamous Burma Railway in 1943. Sadly, my mother was not notified of his death until July 1945. Until then he'd been declared missing in action. I'd been working as a junior clerk for the Queensland Railway Department since the age of fourteen.

There were forty-eight of us in 32 Platoon 'G' Company, which was a Signals Platoon, Royal Australian Corps of Signals. After some six weeks of drill, weapons training, etc, we began our Corps training which was really interesting as it entailed operating radio sets and field telephones plus learning Morse code. After a while we provided communication from radio vans for the Battalion on various Exercises. Often I was called on to assist in the Orderly Room as I had shorthand and typing skills from my job with the Railway Department.

Once our 98 days were completed I was allocated to the 7th Infantry Brigade Sig Troop at Kelvin Grove as a Radio Operator Wireless and Line. We provided communications for the Brigade HQ down to Battalion HQ level. When my National Service obligation was completed I signed up for the CMF and stayed on for 20 years, completing almost 25 years of Service in the Army.

I was transferred from Brisbane to Townsville with the Railway in 1972 and as there was no Signal Unit there, I joined the 31st Infantry Battalion, serving until retirement due to shift work. I enjoyed Army life after National Service and would like to see it reintroduced in some form which would probably eliminate a lot of social problems existing in our society today.

I was instrumental in helping form the Townsville Branch of the National Servicemen's Association of Australia in 1996 and have remained an active member ever since, being Secretary of the Branch for the past 12 years.

JUNGLE SCOUT

Ian (Gilly) Williams

I was called-up for National Service in 1970, but as I was studying to be an electrician it was deferred until 1971. After recruit and Corps training for six months at Singleton Camp in New South Wales, I was sent to 6RAR based on Singapore Island, where we were moved from barracks to barracks.

We had many exercises in the Malayan jungle where I was a forward scout for about eighteen months. During that time one of our blokes got lost in the jungle but luckily we found him.

Ian (Gilly) Williams (right) and Joe McDonald 5 Pl. 'B' Coy 6 RAR, on the move from Selarang Barracks Singapore, 1971.
Photo courtesy I. Williams

A COOK'S STORY

Anthony F. Caruana

Being conscripted into the Army in the 1960's was something that I, unlike others, was looking forward to. I had a learning disability – Dyslexia, which was unknown back then. Because I'd failed 11 years of school, I was classed as being a dumb child. Having already served 18 months in the CMF (42 RQR in Mackay), I believed that being in the Army was where I would be able to get an education. So it was that in July 1968 (13th Intake) I was conscripted into the army as a Nasho. I reported for duty at Northern Command Personnel Depot, Ashgrove, Brisbane and from there went to the 3rd Training Battalion, Singleton, NSW.

There were a number of hurdles that I had to straddle, the first was being unable to write proficiently, so I asked others to assist me in completing forms. Then there was my height. You need to be 5ft 3in to be accepted into the Army. I was 5ft 2in but easily solved this by asking the photographer to turn his back to me. I stood on my toes and then said he could now take the photo. Another hurdle was that you needed a Year 8 Education Certificate as a minimum. I had none. They wanted to give me a test but knowing I would fail I asked if I could take the test in the last 2 weeks of training and they agreed. Thanks to a number of my platoon mates who coached me, I passed the test. To be a rifleman you had to sight a target and I could not as I suffered an injury to my right eye when I was 8 years old and had a permanent scratch on the cornea which meant that I could not see a target with clarity. To everyone's joy at the end of recruit training I was allocated to become a cook. My platoon Sergeant said – 'Thank god for that, now we will all be safe'.

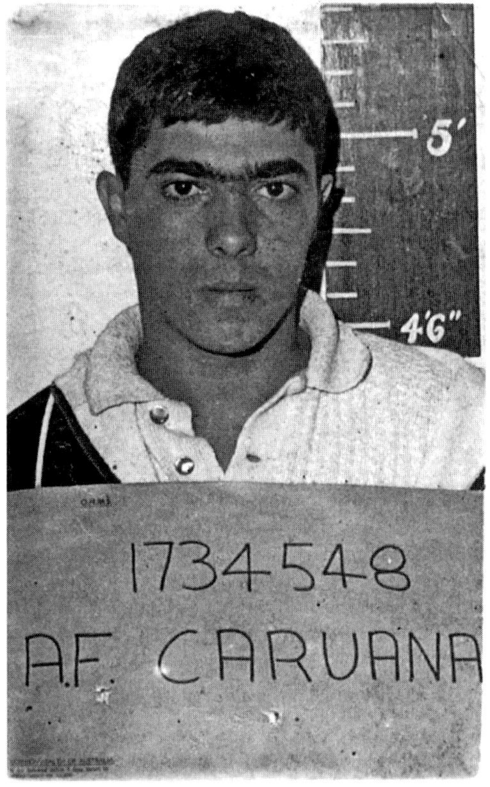

Private Tony Caruana standing on his toes to gain minimum height.
Photo courtesy A. Caruana

At our mid break I elected to go with others to Sydney on Leave. We missed our return bus and were classed as AWOL, then taken to Watson's Bay to wait for new return bookings to be made. We had all made a pact to tell the same story – that we were at the correct location and time given to us. On our return, our Platoon Sergeant warned us that we would be charged with being AWOL. Having been in the CMF I advised my mates that being charged is one thing, but on our evidence as agreed, we should not be found guilty. To the disappointment of our Pl Sgt no charge was recorded against us. But didn't he make us suffer through additional chores such as scrubbing the toilets with a tooth brush, painting the rocks white and polishing the kitchen copper pipes until they looked like new.

Being a Nasho meant that you would return to your home State, in my case Queensland, for your IET (Initial Employment Training). This would be 12 weeks and as I was to be a cook I was off to Wacol just outside Brisbane. Now I was faced with another hurdle. Due to my learning disability I was deemed to be a slow learner. So again I was threatened to be discharged out of the army. Thankfully, an Australian Army Catering Corp instructor, WO2 Archie Clapham, saw potential in me from a practical point. I was the eldest son of 12 children and had learnt to cook from my Mum. He convinced his superiors to give me a go.

Trainee cooks Wacol, 1968. (Tony Caruana 2nd from left.)
Photo courtesy A. Caruana

On weekends under Archie's guidance, through extra tuition, training and a lot of practice, I passed all practical and written tests and qualified as a cook. I then received a posting order to my first unit – The School of Military Survey at Bonegilla, Victoria, which is near Albury/Wodonga. I served the remainder of my National Service there and continued serving in the Australian Army Catering Corp for a total of 20 full-time years and 10 years part-time, exiting as a Warrant Officer First Class – Catering Supervisor.

NASHO MARCHING SONG

Oh we're a pack of bastards
Bastards are we
We'd rather shag than shoot
For Vic-tor-ree

(Origin unknown)

A GUARD OF HONOUR

Ron Keelan

After being selected for National Service in the Air Force, I was assigned to 'B' Flight at RAAF Fairbairn in Canberra from January to June 1956. During that time 'B' Flight was part of a Guard of Honour for General James H. Doolittle of the US Air Force when he visited Canberra that year.

'B' Flight NSW Guard of Honour for US General, James H. Doolittle, RAAF Fairbairn, 1956. *Photo courtesy R.Keelan*

For those readers who have not heard of General Doolittle, I should explain. Shortly after the Japanese attack on the American Pacific fleet at Pearl Harbour, the then Lieutenant Colonel Doolittle commanded a force of sixteen B-25B bombers on what became known as the Doolittle Raid.

Launched from the aircraft carrier *USS Hornet* the raid on the Japanese mainland was a daring and hazardous mission. As Doolittle explained, 'It was to give the folks at home the first good news that we'd had in World War 2. It caused the Japanese to question their warlord. And, from a tactical point of view, it caused the retention of aircraft in Japan for the defence of the home island when we had no intention of hitting them again seriously in the near future. Those planes would have been much more effective in the South Pacific where the war was going on.'

Tokyo, Kobe and Yokahama were bombed and although little damage was done it was a huge embarrassment for the Japanese High Command. The raid was not without cost to the Americans, however, most of the crews survived. A movie about the raid, *'30 Seconds Over Tokyo'*, was made in 1944 with Spencer Tracy playing the part of General Doolittle.

RAAF Base Fairbairn ceased operating as an Air Force base in June 1998 and was sold to the Capital Airport Group.

Aerodrome Defence. *Photo courtesy R. Keelan*

Air Force Nasho Ron Keelan. *Photo courtesy R. Keelan*

RAAF Fairbairn, Canberra, 1956. *Photo courtesy R. Keelan*

MESSING ABOUT

Max E. Schmidt

My National Service began on 9 August, 1955 when the troop train, originating at Cunnamulla and travelling through Charleville and Roma, arrived in Toowoomba to collect the Toowoomba and some of the Darling Downs recruits. Most of the far western blokes who had been on the train for 48 hours were wild lads from grazing stations and rural employment. Some, if not most, of these potential soldiers were wearing the 'wobbly boot' and were very loud and raucous, still with bottles of alcohol in their possession. By the time the train got to Wacol, some of these fellows had demolished and trashed the toilet cubicle in the last carriage.

Upon disembarking at Wacol, we were all lined up on the platform by the Officers who demanded we all contribute five pounds for restitution. Fortunately we all had that amount of money. Only enough trucks were provided for all those whose surnames started with A and going to R. The rest of us had to walk. This system of transport selection operated for almost the entire time we were at Wacol.

The first morning I went to the wrong Mess and was served rolled oats porridge by the earlier recruits who had arrived a week before to train as cooks. This porridge consisted of 5 golf ball-sized blobs, wet on the outside and bone dry in the middle.

During my time in Wacol, I enjoyed the company of fellow Nashos. We played cards and sport and many a good night was spent with me playing guitar and folks from our own and other huts joining in for a sing-song.

I, like all recruits from this National Service scheme, later attended fortnightly Camps at Greenbank and Canungra, as well as obligatory attendance for two years at CMF parades in Toowoomba.

I have been a Member (and my wife Barbara, an Associate Member) of the Toowoomba Branch of The National Servicemen's Association for the past ten years or so. During this time I served for a few years as The Welfare Officer, and Barbara with her Committee, served as the Social Convenor for a longer period.

The following Battalion Journal extracts aptly describe Army life at Wacol while I was there and provide some military humour as well.

LET US BE CLEAR ABOUT THREE FACTS.

FIRSTLY, ALL BATTLES AND ALL WARS ARE WON IN THE END BY THE INFANTRY.

SECONDLY, THE INFANTRYMAN ALWAYS BEARS THE BRUNT. HIS CASUALTIES ARE HEAVIER, HE SUFFERS GREATER EXTREMES OF DISCOMFORT AND FATIGUE THAN THE OTHER ARMS.

THIRDLY, THE ART OF THE INFANTRYMAN IS LESS STEREOTYPED AND FAR HARDER TO ACQUIRE IN MODERN WAR THAN THAT OF ANY OTHER ARM.

FIELD MARSHAL WAVELL.

LIFE IN THE INFANTRY

"The men of 'Able,' 'Baker,' and 'Fox' Companies, and 9 Platoon of 'Charley' Company are all training as Infantrymen. In these pages we gather together some of their comments on their new way of life.

"First we have a poem by 'An Infantryman' of 27 Platoon, 'Fox' Company. I'm not at all sure whether he's 'fair dinkum' or whether my leg is being gently pulled.

'We of the Infantry like this life,
We never ever get into strife,
Our outfit is always spick and span,
And life always runs according to plan.
'Our meals are among the best to get,
And although a lot of jokers fret
Because they do not get enough,
The eats they get make 'em really tough.
'Our Officers are a learned mob,
And they really do an excellent job
In teaching us to drill and fight,
And helping us to see the light.'

Private B. J. Jordan, of 7 Platoon, "Baker" Company, in the following article on the National Service Trainee, gives us an insight into the life and thinking of these young soldiers.

"When an Australian youth reaches 18 years of age, he realises that the time has come when he must become a National Service Trainee.

Th N.S. Trainee is just an ordinary bloke, who, for three months of his life, becomes a little different; for during these three months he has his first look at Army life.

Up until now he has relished his civvy life, doing his ordinary day's work, wearing his own loud ties, walking out with his local girl, in fact, being absolutely normal. However, from the day he arrives at camp, things start to happen, and he starts to change.

He no longer goes to his meal as he pleases; he has to queue for it. He no longer hops out of bed into his clothes, and off to work; in camp he makes his bed, a task abhorred by most; sweeps his hut, equally abhorrent, and what perhaps hurts most of all, shaves daily.

The Trainee loves leave, mess parades, Sunday, and knocking-off time. On the other hand he hates inspections, picks and shovels, bawling C.S.M.'s, and, most of all Reveille.

But there is more to the Trainee's life than just that. When he dons that uniform he has a feeling of pride, and this pride lies in the fact that the uniform he is wearing was perhaps worn by a brother who never came back from the Second World War. Most of all he is wearing the uniform of the Australian Army, an Army of which we are all proud.

And so you see, on the day a Trainee marches out, he is a different man from the one who marched in.

11 Battalion Journal page 16, Intake 3/55.

Life In the Infantry (Contd.)

The lads, of course, relish a good joke and here is a selection of those passed on to me by our happy Infantrymen.

Twenty-seven Platoon in "Fox" Company tell this one:—

"The Company was attentively watching a film, 'The Infantry!' The scene showed a Division making a determined attack on an enemy position. Suddenly there was a breakdown and the area was plunged into darkness. 'What's happened?' came a voice from the front. From the back came the reply, 'They've stopped to polish their brass.'"

Some 27 Pl. lads enjoying a sing-song in their hut.

From the same Platoon comes this conversation piece, "Hello, Corporal, what do you think of the weather?"

"Awful, sir, awful."

"And how's the wife?"

"Just the same, sir."

Then, of course, there are the inevitable American and Australian stories. Pte. J. F. Dalzell, of 27 Platoon, tells this one:—

"An Australian took an American tourist up into the mountains and told him to listen while he shouted, 'Oi!' After some minutes they heard the echo. 'There,' said the Australian, 'you can't beat that in your country.' 'Can't we?' said the American. 'Listen, where I live I stick my head out of the bedroom window and shout, 'Hi there,' before I go to bed. Eight hours later the echo wakes me up."

Pte. C. Cooper tells this one in which the roles are reversed:—

"One day an American and an Australian were talking about big buildings. The American said, 'We have a building in the States so high that you can't see the top for the clouds.' The Australian laughed, 'That's nothing. In Sydney we have a building so high that if a baby fell out of the top window, he would be able to put in for the old age pension by the time he reached the bottom.'"

And here's an interesting conversation piece from 26 Platoon:—

"Do you know why our Sergeant goes to bed dog-tired each night?"

"Because he barks at us all day."

Pte. N. W. Ashmore, of 25 Platoon, tells this one:—

"A troop of rookies were being given a friendly lecture by the Company Commander. During the course of the lecture he asked one lad, 'Well, soldier, what would you like to be in this Army?' With a grin the lad replied 'A returned soldier, Sir.'"

11 Battalion Journal page 18, Intake 3/55.

ACCIDENTS WILL HAPPEN

Brian Smith (Flight Lieutenant)

In mid 1951 I commenced my National Service as a trainee at RAAF Richmond, which is north-west of Sydney near the foot of the Blue Mountains. After six weeks of basic training some of us were chosen to do the Aircrew Course at nearby Schofields. We were interviewed and given aptitude tests which resulted in 9 trainees being chosen for pilot training, the remainder were aircrew. I was one of the lucky ones. Pilot training was both theoretical and practical – learning to fly, firstly in Tiger Moths, then Wirraways before progressing to Vampire and Gloucester Meteor 15 jets.

One day during an Advanced Operations Flying training exercise with air-to-ground rockets, I accidentally pulled the communication plug from its socket. The instructor up front was a verbose Officer who gave long-winded instructions. As I put the plug back in I heard him say 'fire', so I fired off both rockets. The rockets for training purposes had concrete (yes concrete) warheads. He let me know in no uncertain terms that the word 'fire' was part of his talk and not a command.

We were flying over what was then bushland between Badgerys Creek and Camden south-west of Sydney and didn't think any damage had been done. On return to Richmond the instructor and I had to report to the Wing Commander. After I explained the 'accident', we were informed that I had made a direct hit on a poultry farm. One row of hen houses was demolished and a second row badly damaged.

We were ordered to drive out to the farm, tell the poultry farmer the cause of the 'accident' and that the Air Force would pay compensation for the damage. After listening to my story the farmer exclaimed, 'Good God, we're not safe anywhere!' I was docked my Flying Allowance pay for 'poor airmanship' as punishment.

Following completion of National Service, I joined the Citizens Air Force (RAAF Reserve) for three years.

AC2 Brian Smith, RAAF Schofields NSW, 1951.
Photo courtesy B. Smith

HARD LESSONS AT HOLSWORTHY

Don Macleod

When I did my three months National Service in the last Intake at Holsworthy Army Camp NSW in 1957, I was one of the oldest trainees in 22 Platoon, 'E' Company, 12 Battalion. This was because my service had been deferred due to being an apprentice electrician.

Assigned as a gunner (gnr), the first month was spent doing basic training which included marching drill, rifle handling, PT, and work details e.g. kitchen duty, garden cleanup, etc. That led to my first big lesson in the army which is, NEVER VOLUNTEER! On work detail one day we were asked by our Sergeant, 'Who is the best driver among you lot?' I piped up enthusiastically, 'I am'. He then replied, 'OK, in that case you can drive the wheelbarrow all day.'

The next month was taken up with more advanced training such as .303 rifle and Bren gun shoots on the long range as well as Owen gun on the short range. There was also practice grenade throwing, rifle bayonet drill and gas training, which led to another hard lesson, DON'T MAKE SMART REMARKS!

One day we had to attend gas training and after a lecture on the subject we placed canvas covers around one of the toilet blocks which had a lattice surround. This made the toilet block fairly airtight inside. We were then supplied with gas masks and after donning them, marched into the sealed toilet whereupon the officer-in-charge released cans of tear gas. We had to walk around in circles until we were told to take the masks off to sample the effect of the gas.

Some idiot said, 'That's not too bad really', so the Officer released more cans of tear gas. We all ran outside coughing and rubbing our eyes, which was the worst thing to do. We spent the rest of the afternoon continually washing our faces and eyes.

As we were an Artillery Regiment the third month was taken up training on the 25 pounders and associated equipment. I trained on numbers 12 and 62 radio sets for communications between the guns and forward observation positions. There was also advanced marching with rifle in full dress uniform for the Cock-of-the-Walk Competition between companies, and front gate sentry duty plus further long range shoots with rifle and Bren gun.

Gunner Don Macleod (left) 22 Platoon 'E' Company. Last Intake at Holsworthy, 1957. *Photo courtesy D.Macleod*

Finally, we got to throw live grenades! This was a 'real experience' which scared some of the trainees. We had to practice by lobbing a dummy grenade over a crossbar, similar to a football crossbar only higher, and land it in a 44 gallon drum about 15 to 20 yards away. I got quite good at it with dummy grenades but when it came to the real thing it was a different story.

The Sergeant handed me the grenade, I went into the routine – 1,2,3, pulled the pin while holding the lever firmly down, stretched back my arm, lobbed it the best I could AND WATCHED MESMERISED. A hand reached up, grabbed my shoulder roughly and pulled me down while a voice screamed out, 'Get down you idiot'. My Sergeant had saved the day...and me!

About two weeks before we were to finish our time, we were told that the Government had cancelled National Service. We were the last to do three months in the Army at Holsworthy. For the remainder of our time we sat around playing cards and taking it easy.

All in all it was an interesting and enjoyable experience, learning new skills and making new friends, so much so, that I continued in the CMF for the next nine years.

A CMF STORY

Robert Prewitt

After basic training we were required to serve 2 years' part-time in the CMF. At a fortnight camp at Singleton in 1955, my mate and I had local Leave one Friday night.

Catching a bus to town we popped into a pub intending to have a quiet drink before going to a dance in the hall opposite the hotel. However, the night didn't quite turn out the way we expected.

Some regular army blokes in the bar dared us to drink the shelf. Stupidly, we accepted the challenge and got down to some serious boozing. The outcome was we got blind drunk then staggered across the road to the dance. We didn't miss much though.

On one side of the hall were diggers from camp in summer uniform. On the other side they were wearing kilts. There was only a handful of local girls dancing with local boys.

For a joke my mate crossed the dance floor and asked one of the blokes in a kilt for a dance. However, it was taken as an insult and a wild brawl started with both sides joining in. In the midst of the pandemonium my mate and I ducked out a side door and caught the bus back to camp laughing our heads off.

MAD MAX

Ken Shadie

July 1954 and I'm getting ready to report for National Service in the Royal Australian Air Force.

Mum is helping me pack...

'Mum I'm not taking a dressing gown!'

'But you'll be in a hut with other boys...'

'Mum I'm not taking a dressing gown...no way...end of story!'

I join a steam train at Hawkesbury Station heading north. On board a lot of other young blokes heading north as well.

We get off at Awaba Railway Station and are bussed to No. 2 N.S.T Wing RAAF Rathmines on the shores of beautiful Lake Macquarie...our home for next six months.

We are herded into 'Flights', 20 blokes to a hut. I grab a bed and start unpacking.

Bloody hell! There on top of my case...that dressing gown! A horrible brown looking thing with a golden cord tie, my dear Mum has sneaked into my bag.

The other fellers zero in on it. Thinking quickly I say... 'Okay, which one of you clowns put this in my bag?'

It doesn't work. I shove it in my wardrobe swearing never to wear it.

Before we went in some boofhead had written to the newspapers saying National Service is a 'bludge'. The Brass decide to make sure the next Intake (us) work hard and find out exactly what life in the military is all about.

Dawn to dusk we are on the go. It's called 'aerodrome defence' but we're really the army...everything from drill to bayonet charging, dismantling the Bren...you name it we're doing it 7 days a week.

Some blokes try to escape by joining the Band. The Band becomes fifty strong. A well turned out impressive group, who march on parade to the sound of about three bugles. The rest blowing like mad but nothing coming out...a joke but they get out of the hard slog.

With visions of flying Spitfires, and Churchill's stirring speech of 'the few' ringing in our ears, the rest of us apply for Air Crew.

I sit through my interview for Air Crew absolutely terrified that I'll be selected.

The Wing Commander eyeballs me...

'Have you ever been in an aeroplane, son?'

'No'

'Next!'

My best mate is a loveable rat-bag called Max. Max sleeps in the bed next to me and we become great mates sharing lots of laughs.

A couple of months pass and our C.O., Wing Commander Brill D.S.O. D.F.C., decides in the interests of good relations, we need to 'inter-act' more with the local community. (Obviously he's unaware of the local girls hanging around the back gate.)

The good Wing Commander decides to accept a challenge from the Toronto Boxing Club to stage a boxing tournament on the base between the local pugs and we Nashos.

Volunteers are called for and my mad mate Max puts his hand up.

He's never had a fight in his life but he wants to enter the tournament.

'I want you to be my trainer,' he tells me.

'What are you talking about?' I ask.

'I need to get used to being hit in the face.'

Max wants to stand there while I keep hitting him in the face so he can get used to it!

I tell him...as long as he doesn't hit back I'm prepared to do it.

We go into a vigorous training routine which entails Max sticking out his chin and me trying to hit it.

Comes the big day. A hanger is set up with a boxing ring, seats arranged, the crowd is in, and we are ready to take on the Toronto boys.

There's only one problem.

'Has anyone got a dressing gown?'

The boxing tournament is a circus. The only highlight of the night is the appearance of my dressing gown being worn by everyone from 'Lofty' to skinny Max.

It brings great laughter between bouts.

Max, trained to perfection, comes dancing out shaping up like Joe Louis, gets hit flush on the chin, and goes down for the count.

My six months in the RAAF was the best of times.

When we passed out in November that year some of Wing Commander Brill's Address still resonates with me...

'In July, 450 young Australians arrived at Rathmines to carry out their National Service training. They came from all States and formed the largest Intake ever to be trained at an Air Force unit.

On December 4, those same young Australians will march out of Rathmines the better for their service in the Air Force. Broadened and matured by their associations and the loyalty and discipline taught them at Rathmines. Healthier, stronger, better equipped for their civilian careers, better citizens.'

We left the camp promising to keep in touch.

'We should meet up every year.'

'Yeah, let's do that.'

'I'll give you a ring.'

'Let's stay in touch.'

Of course we never did, but I still remember them all fondly.

As for that dressing gown, I left it in the wardrobe. For all I know it's still there.

CONCLUSION

The camaraderie enjoyed by members of the National Servicemen's Association of Australia says a lot about their compulsory military service in the years between 1951 and 1972. Whether they were one of the 6,862 who served in the Navy, one of the 23,500 who served in the Air Force, or one of over a quarter of a million who served in the Army, most would agree it had a big influence on their life.

For the majority that influence was for the good. However, sadly, a number of Nashos who served in war zones overseas have been left suffering from injuries, and problems such as PTSD (Post Traumatic Stress Disorder). Further, in addition to the 212 National Servicemen killed and the 1479 wounded in action, there were deaths and injuries from training and service accidents, not to mention those who were exposed to defoliants in Vietnam, or radiation resulting from the Atomic Bomb tests in Australia during the 1950's.

Nashos have served, and many continue to serve, their country well. They grew up in a society that put responsibility ahead of rights and took the rough with the smooth.

If Australia is to remain the great nation inherited from earlier generations, it would pay to recall those inspiring words spoken by U.S. President John F. Kennedy in his 1961 Inaugural Address, '...ask not what your country can do for you – ask what you can do for your country.'

Ronald Parsons

Toowoomba Qld. 2014

Centenary of 1914-1918 Great War

THE NATIONAL SERVICE HONOUR ROLL

BORNEO

No.	NAME	STATE	UNIT	DIED
5713692	Mills Geoffrey F	WA	22 Const Sqdn	1966
ENLISTED UPON CALL-UP				
3787083	Bridgland Reginald N	Vic	22 Const.Sqdn	1966
TOTAL BORNEO				**2**

VIETNAM

No.	NAME	STATE	UNIT	DIED
2786017	Abbott Dal E	NSW	1RAR	1968
4718946	Abraham Dennis E	SA	104 Signals Squadron	1968+
4719565	Abraham Richard J	SA	9RAR	1969
2784699	Allen Norman G	NSW	7RAR	1967
2784162	Annesley Frederick J	NSW	1RAR	1968
2788583	Archer Gary A	NSW	9RAR	1969
2781363	Arnold Peter J	NSW	6RAR	1967
1730888	Ashton William J	Qld	6RAR	1967
2794278	Attwood Trevor J	NSW	HQ1ATF	1971
2786313	Bailey Errol J	NSW	1RAR	1968.
6709107	Banfield David J	Tas	5RAR	1969.
5715206	Barnett Stuart J	WA	4RAR	1968
2782555	Bartholomew Glen T	NSW	1 Field Squadron	1967
5718195	Beilken Brian C	WA	4RAR	1971
5714453	Bell Alec E	WA	7RAR	1968
5714249	Bell Ronald J	WA	2RAR	1967
2781899	Birchell Michael J	NSW	6RAR	1967
1734408	Black Trevor R	Qld	9RAR	1969
2782525	Bracewell Dennis H	NSW	6RAR	1967
2782812	Brady Gregory V	Qld	1 Field Squadron	1967
2789684	Bramble Peter J	NSW	1 Field Squadron	1969
2785180	Brett William J	NSW	2RAR	1967
6708915	Brewer Kevin F	Tas	4RAR	1968
3787889	Brooks Dennis L	Vic	1 Field Squadron	1967
3794895	Brown Allen R	Vic	6RAR	1969
3790530	Brown Lindsay N	Vic	3RAR	1968
2794031	Bullman John H	NSW	1ARU	1970
2786525	Byrne Robert A	NSW	4RAR	1969+
2787278	Campbell John A	NSW	3RAR	1968
5716427	Cassano Nicola J	M	5RAR	1969
4719003	Caston Robert J	SA	3RAR	1968
4721369	Chapman Rodney S	SA	2RAR	1971
5713804	Clark Donald M	SA	5RAR	1967
3794556	Clark Raymond D	M	6RAR	1970
6708750	Coombs Geoffrey J	Tas	1 Field Squadron	1968
1731426	Cox James G	Qld	7RAR	1967

2787020 Cox Raymond J	NSW	1RAR		1968
5716239 Crouch Noel V	WA	7RAR		1970
2785238 Cutcliffe Timothy J	NSW	2RAR		1967

2788283 Davidson Barry N	NSW	3RAR		1968
3788300 Deed Ramon J	Vic	1 Field Squadron		1967.
3791033 Desnoy John W	Vic	3RAR		1968
4718756 De Vries Van Leeuwen Thomas J	M	3RAR		1968
5715633 Dewar Keith I	WA	3 Cavalry Regiment		1969
2792089 Dickson Stephen W	NSW	7RAR		1970
3789770 Doherty John A	Vic	3RAR		1968
1730929 Drabble Glenn A	Qld	6RAR		1966
2794265 Driscoll Roger W	NSW	HQ1 Task Force		1971
3799449 Duff James	Vic	4RAR		1971
1735143 Duffy Kenneth A	Qld	6RAR		1970
2792150 Dufty Milton R	NSW	7RAR		1971
5716228 Duncuff Alan L	WA	1 Field Squadron		1969

1732701 Evans Paul	Qld	1RAR		1968
3794256 Evans Thomas A	Vic	9RAR		1969

3786921 Farren Leslie T	Vic	5RAR		1966
2787344 Fisher David J	NSW	3SAS		1969
4718368 Fisher Roger L	NSW	3RAR		1968
1731113 Fraser John	Qld	3RAR		1968

3793157 Gaffney Ronald J	NSW	9RAR		1968
1730941 Gant Kenneth H	Qld	6RAR	Long Tan	1966
2789508 George Barry R	NSW	9RAR		1969
5715657 Gibbs Ian J	WA	1RAR		1968
3790395 Gillard Robert J	Vic	3 Cavalry Regt		1968
6708763 Godden Guy R	Tas	3 RAR		1968
1734847 Goody Phillip R	Qld	8RAR		1970
2787716 Graham Samuel	M	4RAR		1969
2782127 Green George B	NSW	5RAR		1967
2791447 Greene John G	NSW	1 Field Squadron		1969
1730947 Grice Victor R	Vic	6 RAR	Long Tan	1966

3791920 Hannaford Michael J	Vic	1 Armoured Reg		1968
2781944 Hart Peter R	NSW	6RAR		1967
3789232 Hawker Norman V	Vic	7RAR		1967
2794350 Hill Donald C	NSW	HQ 1 Task Force		1971
3786634 Holland Tony	M	1 APC Squadron		1966
3794544 Holloway John W	NSW	9RAR		1969
2787776 Houston Kenneth R	NSW	3RAR		1968
2791326 Hurst Harold W	NSW	1 Field Squadron		1970
6708488 Hyland Francis A	Tas	2RAR		1967

2789790 Jackson Peter J	NSW	5RAR		1969
2781847 Jewry Jack	NSW	6RAR	Long Tan	1966

4720992 Kavanagh Graham R	SA	7RAR		1970
1733818 Kermode Raymond C	Qld	9RAR		1969
1734754 Kingston Ian W	Qld	6RAR		1969
1735712 Kowalski Peter F	Qld	2RAR		1971
2782226 Knight Gordon	NSW	6RAR		1966

2781704 Large Paul A	NSW	6RAR	Long Tan	1966
4720583 Larsson Stanley G	SA	7RAR		1970
1734491 Linton Matthew P	NSW	5RAR		1969

2791437 Lisle Anthony	Qld	1 Field Squadron		1969
3797086 Lloyd Allan L	ACT	7RAR		1970
2784015 Lloyd Richard E	NSW	5RAR		1967
3794096 Loughman Matthew	NSW	HQ1ALSG		1969
1730993 McCormack Albert F	Tas	6RAR	Long Tan	1966
1730994 McCormack Dennis J	SA	6RAR	Long Tan	1966
2782440 McDuff Peter E	NSW	2RAR		1967
2787478 McGuire Raymond A	NSW	4RAR		1969
3795935 MacLennan Larry J	Vic	8RAR		1970
3794377 McMillan James C	NSW	5RAR		1969
2785033 McMillan Ross C	NSW	7RAR		1968
5715701 McPherson Lyall H	WA	9RAR		1969
5716533 McQuat John L	WA	8RAR		1970
3793137 Manicola Joseph G	Vic	1ARU		1969
2794496 Mathers Ian G	Qld	12 Field Regt.		1971
5714739 Mathews Geoffrey F	WA	3RAR		1968
2788798 Meredith Thomas F	NSW	9RAR		1969
1731013 Mitchell Warren D	Qld	6RAR	Long Tan	1966
4717751 Mitchinson Kevin L	SA	3 Cavalry Regiment		1967
3795756 Morgan John L	Vic	2AOD		1970
1732186 Morrison Dayle W	Qld	2RAR		1968
2787512 Muc Michael	M	4RAR		1968
2788085 Muller Hans L	M	5RAR		1969
3795712 Munday Barry J	Vic	8RAR		1970
2788524 Murray Peter E	NSW	1RAR		1968
2792729 Navarre Paul J	Vic	7RAR		1970
1735386 Neal Dennis W	Qld	2RAR		1970
4718427 Nelson Dennis E	SA	2RAR		1967
3798081 Niblett Ralph J	Vic	4RAR		1971
4717546 Noack Errol W	SA	5RAR		1966
2787793 Noonan Michael J	NSW	4RAR		1968
2786748O'Brien John A	NSW	1RAR		1968
2782779 O'Hara John L	NSW	1 Field Squadron		1967
5717657 Pengilly Bernard M	WA	4RAR		1971
6709611 Penneyston Peter L	Tas	1 Field Squadron		1970
3789447 Perrin Robert G	Vic	7RAR		1968
2784043 Pearce John G S	NSW	1RAR		1968
1733375 Petersen Victor N	Qld	4RAR		1969
3790094 Pettit Noel C	Vic	2RAR		1967
4719545 Phillips Reginald A	SA	9RAR		1969
3789448 Plain Douglas B	Vic	HQ1 Task Force		1968
4719981 Plane Bruce J	SA	9RAR		1969
3786644 Pomroy Victor I	Vic	3 Cavalry Regiment		1967
3795605 Poulson Daryl	Vic	8RAR		1970
2790170 Power Robert E	NSW	6RAR		1970
2782783 Powter Douglas R J	NSW	6RAR		1965
1734329 Prior Kevin J	Qld	9RAR		1969
3787580 Purcell Anthony T	Vic	6RAR		1966
4719160 Quigley Anthony V	SA	3RAR		1968
1733037 Ramsay Joseph S	Qld	4RAR		1969
2787069 Rands John M	NSW	1RAR		1968
3793403 Reidy Paul F	Vic	9RAR		1969
4719818 Remeljej Alexander	SA	5RAR		1969
3788172 Renshaw Terrence J	Vic	1 Field Squadron		1967

2796378 Rhodes Maxwell L	NSW	4RAR		1971
3796110 Richter Philip M	Vic	8RAR		1970
3793978 Robertson Malcolm R	Vic	1ALSG		1969
4718449 Rogers John	SA	2RAR		1968
5715153 Roost Christopher W	WA	4RAR		1968
1731040 Salveron Douglas J	Qld	6RAR	Long Tan	1966
4719367 Scales Grantley J	SA	9RAR		1969
4720852 Schuit Martinus J M	SA	17 Const. Squadron		1970
3791583 Scott Ian J	Vic	12 Field Squadron		1968
1735424 Scott Ian N	Qld	1 Field Squadron		1970
2781465 Sharp Gordon C	NSW	6RAR	Long Tan	1966
3790506 Sheppard Lawrence R	Vic	1RAR		1968
2787079 Slattery John M	NSW	1RAR		1968
3793566 Smith Baron F	Qld	5RAR		1969
3794831 Smith John	Vic	1 Field Squadron		1969
3797613 Smith Noel A	Vic	21 Eng Sppt Tport		1971
2788912 Smith Peter C	NSW	9RAR		1969
2790417 Sorrensen Gordon D	Qld	9RAR		1969
2790070 Stanford Gregory Ian	NSW	6RAR		1969
5718122 Sprigg Roderick J	WA	4RAR		1971
4719232 Steen David J	M	1 Field Squadron		1968
4719573 Sukmanowsky Michael	SA	1ARU		1968
3786696 Sullivan Paul C	NSW	5RAR		1965
3797623 Talbot Alan	M	7RAR		1971
3787987 Taylor Leonard A	NSW	3RAR		1968
2790880 Teeling Wayne E	NSW	5RAR		1969
2786038 Thomson Ian J	NSW	3RAR		1968
3791207 Tinkham John R	Vic	4RAR		1969
4718911 Thomas William M	SA	3RAR		1968
2789920 Thompson Barry J	NSW	5RAR		1970
5713739 Tomas Marian	WA	5RAR		1966
2792254 Towler Michael	M	HQ1 Task Force		1971
3791291 Trimble Bevan M	Vic	1RAR		1968
2792375 Tully Desmond J	NSW	2RAR		1970
4720253 Turner Timothy C	SA	5RAR		1969
3787416 Tweedie Geoffrey L	Vic	6RAR		1967
5715180 Van Rijsewijk Paul R	M	3RAR		1968
2787255 Wallis Alan J	NSW	1RAR		1968
3786978 Warburton Graham F	Vic	5RAR		1966
5716163 Waring Anthony E	M	5RAR		1969
5713981 Waters Brian D	SA	6RAR		1967
5713748 Watson Bryan P	WA	5RAR		1966
5713986 Webster David R	NSW	6RAR		1967
5713751 Webster James C	WA	5RAR		1967
1731955 Weston Leslie J	NSW	2RAR		1967
3787607 Whiston Colin J	NSW	6RAR	Long Tan	1966
5715978 White James M	WA	5RAR		1969
5715189 Williams Archibald S	WA	1RAR		1968
3797671 Willoughby Garry I	Vic	2RAR		1970
4717841 Wilsen Robert P	SA	3 Cavalry Regiment		1967
4718082 Woolford Richard M	SA	2RAR		1967
3790789 Worle Jeffrey T	Vic	3RAR		1968
1732408 Young Alexander H	NSW	104 Signals Squadron		1968
1733095 Young Brian T	Qld	1RAR		1968
1733547 Young Robert G	Qld	3 Cavalry Regiment		1969

M Migrant, State of residence not specified

ENLISTED UPON CALL-UP OR RE-ENLISTED

4718097 Burns Robert	M	4RAR	1968
2786682 Hollis Anthony E	NSW	1 Field Squadron	1970
2783512 Jackson Robert J	NSW	8RAR	1970
4717754 Musicka Harold R	Vic	9RAR	1969
4718855 Paterson David	SA	3RAR	1971
2781563 Rinkin Kerry P	NSW	5RAR	1967
3411951 Wilson Kevin R	Vic	2RAR	1968

Total Enlisted **7**

VOLUNTARY NATIONAL SERVICEMEN

2786939 Langlands Terrance E	NSW	1RAR	1968
1731467 Martin William H	Qld	1RAR	1968
2412362McGarry Peter S	Vic	2RAR	1967
2141115 Patten Raymond B	NSW	7RAR	1971
217961 Pettit Leslie J	NSW	5RAR	1969
1732899 Salzmann Ronald W	Qld	3RAR	1971
Total Voluntary			**6**

TOTAL VIETNAM **210**

Sources:
The Australian : *'500 - The Australians Who Died in Vietnam'*, Supplement August 18 1988
The Australian War Memorial, Canberra
The Army Central Records Office, Melbourne
The Army History Unit, Canberra
The Vietnam Nominal Roll, Department of Veterans' Affairs
National Servicemen's Association of Australia

The last wreath laid at the Dedication of the National Service Memorial, alongside the Australian War Memorial, Canberra, on 8 September 2010. Made with 212 red silk poppies, one for each National Serviceman who died on active service in Borneo and Vietnam, it was laid on behalf of the Governor-General, Her Excellency Quentin Bryce AC, by Mrs Betty Kingston, whose son Ian died in Vietnam, and Miss Isabelle Doherty, whose grandfather John was also killed in Vietnam. *Photo supplied by NASHO NEWS Qld*